FRANCIS BACON

Essays

Introduction by
MICHAEL J. HAWKINS
Reader in History, School of English and
American Studies, University of Sussex

J. M. Dent & Sons Ltd London

© Biographical Note and Introduction
J. M. Dent & Sons Ltd, 1972

All rights reserved
Made in Great Britain
at the
Aldine Press · Letchworth · Herts
for
J. M. DENT & SONS LTD
Aldine House · Albemarle Street · London
First published in this edition 1906
Last reprinted 1975

Hardback ISBN 0 460 10010 6
Paperback ISBN 0 460 11010 1

CONTENTS

Contents

FRANCIS BACON
A Biographical Note

FRANCIS BACON, Lord Verulam and Viscount St Albans, was born in 1561, the most gifted son of Sir Nicholas Bacon, Lord Keeper of the Great Seal, and nephew of Sir William Cecil, later Lord Burghley and Lord Treasurer, the great minister of Queen Elizabeth. In his thirteenth year Bacon was sent with his elder brother to Trinity College, Cambridge, where he first met the Queen, who was impressed by his precocious intellect and was accustomed to call him 'the young Lord Keeper'. In 1576 he entered Gray's Inn and in the same year joined the embassy of Sir Amyas Paulet to France, where he remained until 1579. The death of his father in that year gave an adverse turn to his fortunes and rendered it necessary that he should decide upon a profession. He accordingly returned to Gray's Inn, and was called to the Bar in 1582. Two years later he entered the House of Commons as member for Melcombe, sitting subsequently for Taunton (1586), Liverpool (1589), Middlesex (1593) and Southampton (1597). In the Parliament of 1586 he took a prominent part in urging the execution of Mary Queen of Scots. About 1591 he formed a friendship with the Earl of Essex, from whom he received many tokens of kindness, being presented with a property at Twickenham which he subsequently sold for the substantial sum of £1,800. In 1596 he was made a Queen's Counsel, but missed the appointment of Master of the Rolls. By 1601 Essex had lost the Queen's favour and had raised his rebellion, and Bacon was one of those appointed to investigate the charges against him and examine witnesses, in connection with which, it has been argued, he showed an ungrateful and indecent eagerness in pressing the case against his former friend and benefactor, who was executed on 25th February

Francis Bacon

1601. His later attempt to justify this act may suggest some pricking of conscience on Bacon's part.

The accession of James VI in 1603 gave a favourable turn to his fortunes: he was knighted, and endeavoured to set himself right with the new powers by writing his 'Apologie' of his proceedings in the case of Essex, who had favoured the succession of James. In the first parliament of the new king he sat for St Albans, and was appointed a Commissioner for Union with Scotland.

In 1606, at the age of forty-five, he married Alice Barnham, the daughter of a London merchant, and in 1607 was made Solicitor-General. The following year he entered upon the Clerkship of the Star Chamber, and was in the enjoyment of a large income; but old debts and present extravagance kept him embarrassed. In 1613 he became Attorney-General, in 1616 a Privy Councillor and in 1617 Lord Keeper. In 1618 he was given the more honorific title of Lord Chancellor. He was knighted in 1603, and created Lord Verulam in 1618 and Viscount St Albans in 1621.

Hardly had he reached this final peak when he was charged in Parliament with receiving bribes, an accusation which might be faced by any office-holder in the early seventeenth century, since official salaries were inadequate and dependence on fees and gratuities paid by suitors was widespread. He was sentenced to a fine of £40,000 which was remitted by the king; committed to the Tower during the king's pleasure, although this was that he should be released in a few days; and was barred from holding office or sitting in Parliament. He narrowly escaped being deprived of his titles.

Thenceforth he devoted himself to study and writing, and in March 1626 met his end in the conduct of a scientific experiment. Driving through London on a snowy day, the idea struck him of making an experiment as to the antiseptic properties of snow, in consequence of which he caught a chill which ended in his death. He died leaving debts to the amount of £22,000.

Bacon might well have expected, by birth and ability, a swift rise to the highest offices. By inclination, too, he was a

A Biographical Note

'political animal'; no cloistered scholar, he held that the active life was preferable to the contemplative. Advancement, however, was slow, and his political power never matched that of many statesmen with less clearly developed analytical powers. The intellect of Bacon was one of the most powerful and searching ever possessed by man, and he is claimed by some scientists as the originator of the modern school of experimental research. The most popular of his works is the *Essays*, which convey profound and condensed thought in a style that is at once clear and rich. His moral character was extremely mixed and complex, and bears no comparison with his intellect. Futile attempts, supported sometimes with much ingenuity, have even been made to claim for Bacon the authorship of Shakespeare's plays.

INTRODUCTION

THE career of Francis Bacon was paradoxical. He was born in 1561 into the high administrative class of Elizabethan England and he could expect the highest office, yet by 1603 he had obtained only a reversion of the Clerkship in Star Chamber, which, as he often complained, was poor reward in an age when political advancement depended much on family connections. The belief that man was *faber fortunae*, architect of his fortune,[1] must have been difficult to maintain, but, despite moments of disillusion, he did not abandon, even after his fall in 1621, the hope of political power. Similarly in the field of letters and thought Bacon's early promise had not matured. As an adolescent he had condemned the prevailing philosophical methods and, as a young man, had taken 'all knowledge to be [his] province', but he had published only a pamphlet attacking the Earl of Essex's treason, some religious meditations and the first edition of the *Essays* (1597), consisting of ten brief sketches, mere 'fragments of my conceits'.

As may be seen in the biographical note above, Bacon's reputation in politics, literature and philosophy rests on the achievements of his mature middle age. During the years of his political influence Bacon published the substantial works which make up his *Instauratio Magna*, or Great Renewal of Learning, and a number of other pieces. In 1605 appeared *The Proficience and Advancement of Learning*, expanded and translated by the author into Latin for the international scholarly community as *De Dignitate et Augmentis Scientiarum* in 1623. In 1609 he published *De Sapientia Veterum*, in 1620 the *Novum Organum* and *Parasceve ad Historiam Naturalem et Experimentalem*, in 1622 the *Historia Naturalis et Experimentalis* and *The*

[1] p. 121 below. cf. R. C. Cochrane, 'Francis Bacon and the Architect of Fortune', *Studies in the Renaissance*, vol. v, 1958.

Introduction

Historie of the Raigne of King Henry the seventh, and in 1625
Apophthegmes New and Old. In 1612 and 1625 appeared the
much enlarged and rewritten second and third editions of
the *Essays.* Bacon died in 1626, but the *New Atlantis* and
Sylva Sylvarum were published in 1627 by William Rawley,
his chaplain and early biographer. Many lesser works and
fragments were published later.

Philosophically Bacon was perhaps more successful and
less original in attacking existing ways of thinking than in
establishing new ones. He condemned the *a priori,* syllo-
gistic method [1] and reliance on authority which he had been
taught at Cambridge. Compared with inventions or dis-
coveries like gunpowder, printing or the magnet, the
established philosophies were fruitless; they led to the
spinning of 'cobwebs of learning, admirable for the fineness
of thread and work, but of no substance or profit'. The old
philosophers were like boys, 'prompt to chatter, but in-
capable of generation'. Bacon also attacked empiricists who
pursued induction by simple enumeration and built pre-
carious conclusions, 'exposed to peril from a contradictory
instance'. Men's senses and understanding were beset by
four sorts of Idol: the Idols of the Tribe arose from erroneous
methods of thinking common to humanity as a whole; the
Idols of the Cave from those of the individual; Idols of the
Market Place from popular language and communication;
and Idols of the Theatre from erroneous philosophies. [2]

To Bacon learning ought to be profitable in the sense of
enlarging man's control over his environment; knowledge
was for the 'relief of man's estate'. A new scheme was
proposed in Bacon's *Instauratio Magna. The Advancement
of Learning* outlined existing knowledge, pinpointing its
deficiencies. *The Novum Organum* propounded Bacon's new
epistemology (science of the method or grounds of knowledge). By observation of, or preferably experiment with,

[1] i.e. The method of reasoning from causes to effects, from abstract
notions to their consequences, by means of syllogism (the drawing of a
conclusion supposed to result necessarily from two premisses having a
common term).
[2] The bulk of these attacks is in the first books of *The Advancement of
Learning* (Everyman No. 719) and the *Novum Organum.*

Introduction

the 'instances' of natural phenomena, and careful distinction of positive and negative examples, the 'forms' of nature were ultimately to be discovered. Axioms of greater and greater generality could be established and applied to other situations. Science was thus to become inductive, inferring general laws or principles from the observation of particular instances, although the application of the axioms left room for the exercise of a rational deductive, as opposed to inductive, faculty.

Much controversy has raged about this method and Bacon's general scientific contribution. It has been claimed (and also denied) that Bacon did not give enough weight to the role of hypothesis in framing scientific experiments and that he regarded the collection of data as a mere mechanical process. It is unclear what Bacon meant by a 'form' and how far he had moved from the old scholastic doctrines of 'substance' to a kinematic, mechanistic approach to physics. He was frequently credulous, and ignorant of, or hostile to, significant contemporary scientific developments, which anyway were often based on mathematical, deductive processes of thought rather than Baconian induction. The idea of taking 'all knowledge' into one man's province has been said to be scholastic in the breadth of its claim. The twelfth-century *Book of Sentences* of Peter Lombard has been found to contain the 'Baconian' view that 'the world is made for the sake of man, that it may serve him'. Finally, although Bacon held that 'experiments of light' were more important than 'experiments of fruit', he has been condemned for not appreciating the value of 'pure' knowledge. But Bacon was at least a successful propagandist for a practical, optimistic view of the function of natural philosophy. He foresaw the co-operation of scientists and state patronage of their efforts. Even if the results of induction could never be more than probable, probability could always be refined and it was a sufficient ground for what Bacon most desired—action.

The *Essays* were long thought to be only peripheral to Bacon's main work. Taking their cue from Bacon's own

Introduction

description of the earlier editions as 'recreations of my other studies', many critics held with Arber that the *Essays* 'formed no essential part of his work'.[1] A different view now prevails. The *Essays* were intended to supply many of the deficiencies in the 'moral and civil knowledge' of men as individuals or in society which Bacon indicated in the second book of *The Advancement of Learning*,[2] especially in the most neglected part of civil knowledge, that concerning negotiation or business.[3]

Bacon held that natural philosophy and civil knowledge were analogous and that induction could be applied to ethics and politics.[4] The phenomena of human society, although the 'hardliest',[5] could be reduced to axioms as could those of physics or indeed of law. From the axioms established could follow precepts for action. 'Nature to be commanded must be obeyed' was applicable to human as well as physical nature; knowledge is power and the area of man's authority over himself and his fellows could be extended. Thus Bacon's 'Faustian urge' might be assuaged, although the inquiry could not be finished in his life. Just as Bacon contributed only fragments towards his experimental plan of natural philosophy, so the *Essays* were only a beginning of the study of human relationships. Only by co-operative effort over many generations could the work be completed and made methodical.

Modern liberal opinion has been less certain of the positive moral value of man's control over man than of his control over his physical environment. The Machiavellian overtones of much of Bacon's advice have been stressed and the *Essays* condemned as immoral or at least amoral; 'Good advice from Satan's kingdom' in Blake's words. Bacon approved

[1] Ed. E. Arber, *A Harmony of the Essays, Etc., of Francis Bacon* (English Reprints No. 27, Birmingham, 1871). This is the best edition for comparing the various editions of the *Essays*.

[2] *The Advancement*, especially pp. 170–203 in the Everyman edition.

[3] 'The wisdom touching negotiation or business hath not been hitherto collected into writing, to the great derogation of learning. . . . It is by learned men for the most part despised, as inferior to virtue, and an enemy to meditation' (*ibid.* p. 181).

[4] *Novum Organum*, Book 1, aphorism cxxvii.

[5] *The Advancement*, p. 179.

Introduction

of Machiavelli (1469–1527) for studying 'what men do, and not what they ought to do.[1] This is another example of Bacon's protest against contemporary thinking, which proceeded, in moral as in natural philosophy, deductively and syllogistically, and concentrated on the ideal.

'In the handling of this science, those which have written seem to me to have done as if a man, that professed to teach to write, did only exhibit fair copies of alphabets and letters joined, without giving any precepts or directions for the carriage of the hand or the framing of the letters.' [2]

A viable morality could come only from the subordination of man's appetite and will to reason; to achieve this it was necessary to survey man dispassionately and scientifically.

'It is not possible to join serpentine wisdom with columbine innocency, except men know exactly all the conditions of the serpent. . . . An honest man can do no good upon those that are wicked to reclaim them, without the help of the knowledge of evil. . . . We ought to cast up our account, what is in our power, and what not. . . . The first article of this knowledge is to set down sound and true distributions and descriptions of the several characters and tempers of men's natures and dispositions. . . .' [3]

In particular, moral philosophers had failed to appreciate the variety of human nature; they had 'sought to make men's minds too uniform and harmonical'.[4] Bacon's concern with a practical effective morality is made clear by his 'most compendious' point:

'The most noble and effectual to the reducing of the mind unto virtue and good estate . . . is the electing and propounding unto a man's self good and virtuous ends of his life, *such as may be in a reasonable sort within his compass to attain.*' [5]

In their third edition, the one printed in this volume, the *Essays* had become 'Counsels, Civil and Moral'; they were

[1] *The Advancement*, p. 165.
[2] *Ibid.*, p. 153.
[3] *Ibid.*, pp. 165–8.
[4] *Ibid.*, p. 162.
[5] *Ibid.*, p. 176 (my italics).

Introduction

precepts based on a careful, if incomplete, observation of human nature.

But Bacon did not approach human, any more than physical, nature as a 'little child', his mind a *tabula rasa*. He held that

'There is formed in everything a double nature of good: the one, as everything is a total or substantive in itself; the other, as it is a part or member of a greater body; whereof the latter is in degree the greater and the worthier. . . . The conservation of duty to the public ought to be much more precious than the conservation of life and being.' [1]

The active life was preferable to the contemplative, the active good to the passive, and the advancement and perfecting of things to their mere preservation.[2] The *Essays* presuppose that the public or political life is valuable, and so too is advancement within it. But equally conformity to the established religious and political order is essential. This order might be imperfect, and Bacon was intent on practical reforms to secure it,[3] but the consequences of 'Seditions and Troubles', 'Atheism' or of breaking 'Unity in Religion' were incalculable. Bacon was in the mainstream of European opinion which stressed the value of strong executive power and tended to regard independent centres of authority, whether ecclesiastic, aristocratic or parliamentary, as old-fashioned and disruptive. In abandoning Essex, his former patron, he placed the civil order above any private loyalty, but the *Essays* do not squarely face the possibility that the individual's advancement may be against the interests of the State.

If there was greater ethical concern in Bacon than in Machiavelli, Bacon was Machiavellian in basing morality on secular and civic rather than religious considerations.[4] Whatever he intended, by asserting that the study of God's

[1] *The Advancement*, pp. 155–6.
[2] *Ibid.*, pp. 157–62.
[3] The 'causes and motives' outlined in the essay 'Of Seditions and Troubles' (pp. 42–8 of the present edition) may be taken as an excellent summary of the grievances of Englishmen in the 1620s.
[4] cf. F. Raab, *The English Face of Machiavelli* (London, 1964).

Introduction

works (man and nature) was hardly, if at all, less pious than the study of God's Word as revealed in Scripture, he made possible the attempt to establish human ends in both politics and science. Except in so far as it was a useful social cement, religion might be divorced from politics, as it equally might from natural philosophy in Bacon's scheme.

Bacon did not in fact follow his inductive method when writing the *Essays*. They are highly personal, aphoristic pieces which reveal clearly Bacon's presuppositions.[1] The illustrative material is carefully selected to maintain the points; only when the plan of a piece is deliberately antithetic [2] is there any attempt to balance arguments for and against a position. Bacon uses partly his own and his contemporaries' experiences; this is the nearest he comes to direct observation. Mostly, however, he relies on material from classical and renaissance sources, especially history and biography.

'Lives, if they be well written, propounding to themselves a person to represent in whom actions both greater and smaller, public and private, have a commixture, must of necessity contain a more true, native and lively representation.' [3]

The work of Machiavelli, Commines (1445–1509) and Sarpi (1552–1623) may be traced in the *Essays*, but perhaps Guicciardini (1483–1540) was the modern historian whose influence on Bacon was most potent.[4] Among the ancient authors on whom Bacon relied, the Stoics of the Latin Silver Age (A.D. 17–130), notably Seneca and Tacitus, were particularly important. In some of the *Essays* there is a marked concern with Stoic and Renaissance themes such as

---

[1] Given Bacon's loveless marriage, the essays 'Of Marriage and Single Life' and 'Of Love' (pp. 22–3, 29–30) seem intensely personal. The essay 'Of Deformity' (pp. 131–2) is widely supposed to be a hardly veiled attack on the misshapen Robert Cecil, first Earl of Salisbury, Bacon's cousin and political rival. But in general the *Essays* abound with Bacon's political and social assumptions.

[2] *e.g.* 'Of Simulation and Dissimulation' (pp. 17–19).

[3] *The Advancement*, p. 74.

[4] Especially in the essays 'Of Empire' and 'Of Youth and Age' (pp. 57–61, 127–8). cf. V. Luciani, 'Bacon and Guicciardini', *Publications of the Modern Language Association of America*, vol. 62, 1947.

Introduction

the mutability of human affairs, the 'Vicissitude of Things', and 'Adversity'. This last essay is based on Seneca's 'The good things which belong to prosperity are to be wished; but the good things which belong to adversity are to be admired'.[1] Such concerns may modify some of the bland assertions which have been made of Bacon's optimism.

Bacon was also indebted to the Silver Age for the prose style of the *Essays*. He and his generation fought again the old battle between Ciceronian and Senecan styles, and the *Essays* were a major salvo in the anti-Ciceronian assault, preliminary rounds of which had been fired by Thomas Nashe (1567–1601) and Gabriel Harvey (1545–1630). In Rawley's words, Bacon aimed rather at 'masculine, and clear expression than at any fineness, or affectation of phrases. . . . [He] accounted words to be but subservient or ministerial to matter'. This was another attack on contemporary philosophy which stressed 'words rather than matter'.[2] To Bacon rhetoric was the 'art of applying reason to imagination for the better moving of the will'; that is, its purpose is to induce man to act rationally rather than emotionally. Purely sensuous word schemes designed to give pleasure were adequate if abstract literary eloquence was all that was needed, but for the practical business of life a plainer style which reflected the dispassionate processes of the rational mind was preferable. 'Young students are more satisfied with a flowery easy style than with excellent matter in harsh words.' Yet, although the Royal Society's 'mathematical plainness' of language owed much to Bacon, Bacon's style was far from unadorned. The Senecans stressed 'figures of wit and thought', metaphors, epigrams, aphorisms, antitheses and paradoxes, or, more generally, 'pointed sentences'. Bacon was suspicious of Seneca's verbal ingenuity and preferred Tacitus as a model both for his style and for his 'prudential' political wisdom. But Bacon's first ten brief essays, derived from a commonplace book of aphorisms similar to many kept in the sixteenth century,

[1] pp. 15–16 of the present edition.
[2] cf. Roger Ascham's 'You know not what hurt you do to learning that care not for words, but for matter'.

Introduction

were no more than terse, unconnected and unillustrated maxims. In later editions illustrative material was added and an easier flow achieved,[1] but the emphasis was still on 'significance'. In 1684 Burnet could complain:

'Even the great Sir Francis Bacon, that was the first that writ our language correctly; as he is still our best author, yet in some places has figures so strong, that they could not now pass before a severe judge.'

In neither style nor content did Bacon owe much to Montaigne, the other great contemporary originator of the Essay, whose collection first appeared in 1580. Both were anti-Ciceronians, but Montaigne's diffuse and leisurely style and intimate approach differ greatly from Bacon's terseness and objectivity. It has been suggested that Bacon used Montaigne as a stylistic model more closely in his later essays, but in fact Bacon was capable of writing in a flowing manner from the beginning of his literary career. The style and systematic plan of Bacon's *Essays* were intended to fulfil a specific didactic purpose for which the more reflective mood which later dominated the Essay as a genre was inappropriate. Montaigne's scepticism must be contrasted with Bacon's confidence in man's ability to counter the defects of his understanding, and Montaigne's unwillingness to be involved in politics distinguishes him further from Bacon. Bacon did use a few of Montaigne's ideas, but generally the mere fact that they both called their collections *Essays* has been responsible for the drawing of invidious comparisons between the two when really their aims differed totally.

Bacon's reputation has fluctuated markedly over the years.[2] In this century alone he has been condemned for

[1] The first ten essays were 'Of Studies, Discourse, Ceremonies and Respect, Followers and Friends, Suitors, Expense, Regiment of Health, Honour and Reputation, Faction and Negotiating'. Of these 'Of Followers and Friends' was least changed by the 1625 edition, but most of them retain their original openings and Bacon's early style may be judged there.

[2] An important nineteenth-century attack may be read in Macaulay, *Critical and Historical Essays*, vol. 2 (Everyman No. 226).

Introduction

undermining the Elizabethan 'world picture' by breaking the complex pattern of 'correspondence' which linked the 'microcosm', Man, to the 'macrocosm', God and the Universe; for facilitating the 'dissociation of sensibility' by compartmentalizing reason and faith and thus weakening the analogous and allegorical ways of thinking which the Elizabethan imagination had used so fruitfully; and in general for concentrating on utility rather than morality. Alternatively he has been defended as the prophet of the Industrial Revolution and the 'rise of the middle classes'.[1] Too often such views, whether for or against Bacon, have depended on the particular 'world picture' of the commentator. Not enough attention has been paid to the traditional element in Bacon's thought. We have seen that his natural philosophy was influenced by scholastic presuppositions; he was also strongly affected by contemporary assumptions about the proper hierarchical and paternalistic nature of human relationships in both politics and society at large. The separation of theology and philosophy had long been a grievance against certain trends in later medieval scholasticism typified by William of Ockham (d. *c.* 1349), although his thought had had different consequences from Bacon's. However, Bacon proclaimed himself a radical and we are entitled to judge him as such. He argued that the Elizabethan world picture lacked vitality and could be replaced by a new, strong, coherent one more in touch with 'reality'. The *Essays* were to contribute to that new view; how successful they were the reader must judge.

MICHAEL J. HAWKINS

School of English and American Studies
University of Sussex, 1972

[1] cf. E. M. W. Tillyard, *The Elizabethan World Picture* (1943); B. Willey, *The Seventeenth Century Background* (1934); S. L. Bethell, *The Cultural Revolution of the Seventeenth Century* (1951); L. C. Knights, *Explorations* (1946); B. Farrington, *Francis Bacon, Philosopher of Industrial Science* (1951); C. Hill, *Intellectual Origins of the English Revolution* (1965).

SELECT BIBLIOGRAPHY

COLLECTED WORKS

Works. Ed. J. Spedding, R. L. Ellis and D. D. Heath. 7 vols. 1858–61. Reprinted Stuttgart-Bad Canstatt, 1963, and New York, 1968.
Philosophical Works. Ed. J. M. Robertson. 1905.

SELECTIONS

A Preface to Bacon. Ed. C. J. Dixon, 1963; *Francis Bacon.* Ed. S. Warhaft, Toronto and London, 1965; *Francis Bacon.* Ed. A. Johnston, 1965.

BIBLIOGRAPHIES

Francis Bacon: A Bibliography of his Works and of Baconiana to the year 1750, by R. W. Gibson. Oxford, 1950. Supplement, 1959.
Francis Bacon, 1926–1966, compiled by J. Kemp Houck. Elizabethan Bibliographies Supplements, 1968.

SEPARATE WORKS

Essayes, 1597 (10 essays), 1612 (38 essays), 1625 (58 essays); ed., with notes, E. A. Abbott, 2 vols. 1870; ed., with notes, F. Storr and C. H. Gibson, 1885; ed., with notes, A. S. West, 1899. See also E. Arber, *A Harmony of the Essays,* 1871, for a reprint of the three original editions.
Advancement of Learning, 1605, 1629. Ed. G. W. Kitchin, 1861; W. A. Wright, Oxford, 1868, frequently reprinted; A. Johnston (with *New Atlantis*), Oxford, 1972. In an expanded version, in Latin, as *De Augmentis Scientiarum,* 1623; trans. G. Wats, Oxford, 1640; trans. J. Devey, 1853, 1894 (with *Novum Organum*).
De Sapientia Veterum, 1609. Trans. *The Wisdom of the Ancients,* by A. Gorges, 1619.
Novum Organum, 1620. Ed. G. W. Kitchin, Oxford, 1855; ed. T. Fowler, Oxford, 1878, 1889; trans. and ed. F. H. Anderson, New York, 1960.
New Atlantis (with *Sylva Sylvarum*), 1627. Ed. G. C. Moore Smith, Cambridge, 1900; ed. A. B. Gough, Oxford, 1924.
History of Henry VII, 1622. Ed. J. R. Lumby, Cambridge, 1876.

BIOGRAPHY

Letters and Life, ed. J. Spedding, 7 vols. 1867–74, repr. with Works, 1963, 1968 (includes the speeches).
Biographical studies include T. Fowler, *Bacon,* 1881; R. W.

Select Bibliography

Church, *Bacon*, 1884; E. A. Abbot, *Bacon*, 1885; J. Nichol, *Francis Bacon*, 2 vols., Edinburgh, 1888–9; G. W. Steeves, *Francis Bacon*, 1910; B. Farrington, *Francis Bacon, Philosopher of Industrial Science*, 1951; J. G. Crowther, *Francis Bacon: the First Statesman of Science*, 1960; F. H. Anderson, *Francis Bacon: his career and thought*, Los Angeles, 1962; John Russell, *Francis Bacon*, 1971.

COMMENTARIES

Anderson, F. H. *The Philosophy of Francis Bacon*. Chicago, 1948.

Broad, C. D. *The Philosophy of Francis Bacon*. Cambridge, 1926. Reprinted in *Ethics and the History of Philosophy*. 1952.

Farrington, B. *The Philosophy of Francis Bacon*. Liverpool, 1964 (includes trans. of 'The Masculine Birth of Time', 'Thoughts and Conclusions' and 'The Refutation of Philosophies').

James, D. G. *The Dream of Learning: an Essay on the Advancement of Learning, Hamlet and King Lear*. Oxford, 1951.

Knights, L. C. 'Bacon and the Dissociation of Sensibility', in *Explorations*, 1946.

Lemmi, C. W. *The Classical Deities in Bacon*. Baltimore, 1933.

Padhi, Shanti. *Serpent and Columbine: four chapters on Bacon and the Advancement of Learning*. New Delhi, 1969.

Rossi, Paulo. *Francis Bacon: from Magic to Science*. 1968.

Sessions, W. A. (ed.) *Studies in the Literary Imagination*, iv. 1971, 'The Legacy of Francis Bacon'. Atlanta, Georgia, 1971 (contains 10 articles).

Vickers, B. *Francis Bacon and Renaissance Prose*. Cambridge, 1968 (includes list of modern critical books and articles).

Wallace, K. R. *Francis Bacon on Communication and Rhetoric*. Chapel Hill, 1943.

Wallace, K. R. *Francis Bacon on the Nature of Man: The Faculties of the Soul*. Urbana, 1967.

White, H. B. *Peace Among the Willows: the Political Philosophy of Francis Bacon*. The Hague, 1968 (on the *New Atlantis*).

Whittaker, V. K. *Francis Bacon's Intellectual Milieu*. Los Angeles, 1962.

Periodical Literature: B. Vickers, *Essential Articles for the Study of Francis Bacon*. Hamden, Connecticut, 1968 (reprints 14 articles and lists others), London 1972.

BACKGROUND WORKS

Boas, M. *The Scientific Renaissance, 1540–1630*. 1962, 1970.

Briggs, R. *The Scientific Revolution in the Seventeenth Century*. 1969.

Graig, H. *The Enchanted Glass: the Elizabethan Mind in Literature*. Oxford, 1936, 1950.

Fisch, H. *Jerusalem and Albion: the Hebraic Factor in Seventeenth-Century Literature*. 1964.

Select Bibliography

Gilbert, N. A. *Renaissance Concepts of Method*. New York, 1960, 1963.

Haydn, H. *The Counter-Renaissance*. New York, 1950.

Jones, R. F. *Ancients and Moderns: a Study of the Rise of the Scientific Movement in Seventeenth-Century England*. St Louis, 1936, 1961.

Kearney, H. F. *Origins of the Scientific Revolution*. 1964, 1966.

Willey, B. *The Seventeenth Century Background*. 1934, 1949.

Wilson, F. P. *Elizabethan and Jacobean*. Oxford, 1945.

BACON'S ESSAYS
Bacon's place in the history of English prose style is discussed by Wallace, Knights, Vickers, Fisch and Wilson in the books listed above. Important commentary on and criticism of the *Essays* is to be found in the following articles.

Croll, M. W. A series of articles on seventeenth-century prose, written between 1914 and 1929, now reprinted in *Style, Rhetoric and Rhythm*, ed. J. Max Patrick *et al*, Princeton, 1966.

Crane, R. S. 'The Relation of Bacon's *Essays* to his program for the Advancement of Learning', in *Schelling Anniversary Papers*, New York, 1923. Reprinted in *Essential Articles*.

Zeitlin, J. 'The Development of Bacon's *Essays*'. *Journal of English and Germanic Philology*, 27 (1928).

Walters, M. 'The Literary Background of Bacon's Essay "Of Death"'. *Modern Language Review*, 35 (1940).

Tillotson, G. 'Words for Princes', in *Essays in Criticism and Research*. Cambridge, 1942.

Griffiths, G. S. 'The Form of Bacon's *Essays*'. *English*, 5 (1945).

McMahon, A. P. 'Bacon's Essay "Of Beauty"'. *Publications of the Modern Language Association of America*, 60 (1945).

Cochrane, R. C. 'Francis Bacon and the Architect of Fortune'. *Studies in the Renaissance*, 5 (1958).

Fisch, S. 'Georgics of the Mind: the experience of Bacon's *Essays*'. *Critical Quarterly*, 13 (1971).

Unless otherwise stated the place of publication of books is London

THE TEXT

In 1587 there was published *Essayes. Religious Meditations. Places of perswasion and disswasion. Seene and allowed.* The volume, reprinted in 1598 and 1606, contains ten essays. The Religious Meditations are in Latin ('Meditationes Sacrae'). The *Places of perswasion and disswasion* are entitled 'Coulers of Good and Evill; a fragment'.

The Essaies of Sir Francis Bacon Knight the king's solliciter generall appeared in 1612; reprinted thrice in 1613, and at Edinburgh in 1614 and 1624. This volume contains essays only— 38 in number, 29 of them new, and the rest corrected and enlarged.

The final edition, *The Essayes or Counsels, Civill and Morall, of Francis Lo. Verulam, Viscount St Alban,* was published in 1625; reprinted 1632, 1639, 1664, 1668, etc., and again by various editors during the nineteenth century. It contains 58 essays, 20 of them being new and most of the remainder altered and enlarged.

The text of the present edition is that of 1625; it is reprinted from Vol. VI (1861) of Bacon's collected works, edited by J. Spedding, R. L. Ellis and D. D. Heath, 7 vols., 1858–61.

THE RIGHT HONORABLE

MY VERY GOOD LO.

THE DUKE OF BUCKINGHAM

HIS GRACE, LO. HIGH ADMIRALL
OF ENGLAND

EXCELLENT LO.

SALOMON saies; *A good Name is as a precious oyntment;* And I assure my selfe, such wil your *Graces* Name bee, with Posteritie. For your Fortune, and Merit both, have beene Eminent. And you have planted Things, that are like to last. I doe now publish my *Essayes;* which of all my other workes, have beene most Currant: For that, as it seemes, they come home, to Mens Businesse, and Bosomes. I have enlarged them, both in Number, and Weight; So that they are indeed a New Worke. I thought it therefore agreeable, to my Affection, and Obligation to your Grace, to pre-fix your Name before them, both in English, and in Latine. For I doe conceive, that the Latine Volume of them, (being in the Universall Language) may last, as long as Bookes last. My *Instauration,* I dedicated to the *King:* My *Historie* of *HENRY the Seventh,* (which I have now also translated into Latine) and my *Portions* of *Naturall History,* to the *Prince:* And these I dedicate to your *Grace;* Being of the best Fruits, that by the good Encrease, which *God* gives to my Pen and Labours, I could yeeld. *God* leade your *Grace* by the Hand.

Your Graces most Obliged and
faithfull Servant,

FR. ST. ALBAN.

melancholy and indisposition, and unpleasing to themselves? One of the fathers, in great severity, called poesy *vinum dæmonum*, because it filleth the imagination, and yet it is but with the shadow of a lie. But it is not the lie that passeth through the mind, but the lie that sinketh in and settleth in it, that doth the hurt, such as we spake of before. But howsoever these things are thus in men's depraved judgments and affections, yet truth, which only doth judge itself, teacheth that the inquiry of truth, which is the love-making or wooing of it, the knowledge of truth, which is the presence of it, and the belief of truth, which is the enjoying of it, is the sovereign good of human nature. The first creature of God, in the works of the days, was the light of the sense; the last was the light of reason; and his sabbath work, ever since, is the illumination of his Spirit. First he breathed light upon the face of the matter or chaos; then he breathed light into the face of man; and still he breatheth and inspireth light into the face of his chosen. The poet that beautified the sect that was otherwise inferior to the rest, saith yet excellently well: *It is a pleasure to stand upon the shore, and to see ships tost upon the sea: a pleasure to stand in the window of a castle, and to see a battle and the adventures thereof below: but no pleasure is comparable to the standing upon the vantage ground of truth* (a hill not to be commanded, and where the air is always clear and serene), *and to see the errors, and wanderings, and mists, and tempests, in the vale below:* so always that this prospect be with pity, and not with swelling or pride. Certainly, it is heaven upon earth, to have a man's mind move in charity, rest in providence, and turn upon the poles of truth.

To pass from theological and philosophical truth, to the truth of civil business: it will be acknowledged, even by those that practise it not, that clear and round dealing is the honour of man's nature; and that mixture of falsehood is like allay in coin of gold and silver; which may make the metal work the better, but it embaseth it. For these winding and crooked courses are the goings of the serpent; which goeth basely upon

Of Truth

the belly, and not upon the feet. There is no vice that doth so cover a man with shame as to be found false and perfidious. And therefore Mountaigny saith prettily, when he inquired the reason, why the word of the lie should be such a disgrace and such an odious charge? saith he, *If it be well weighed, to say that a man lieth, is as much to say as that he is brave towards God and a coward towards men.* For a lie faces God, and shrinks from man. Surely the wickedness of falsehood and breach of faith cannot possibly be so highly expressed, as in that it shall be the last peal to call the judgements of God upon the generations of men; it being foretold, that when Christ cometh, *he shall not find faith upon the earth.*

Essay II.—OF DEATH

MEN fear death, as children fear to go in the dark; and as that natural fear in children is increased with tales, so is the other. Certainly, the contemplation of death, as the *wages of sin*, and passage to another world, is holy and religious; but the fear of it, as a tribute due unto nature, is weak. Yet in religious meditations there is sometimes mixture of vanity and of superstition. You shall read in some of the friars' books of mortification, that a man should think with himself what the pain is if he have but his finger's end pressed or tortured, and thereby imagine what the pains of death are, when the whole body is corrupted and dissolved: when many times death passeth with less pain than the torture of a limb; for the most vital parts are not the quickest of sense. And by him, that spake only as a philosopher and natural man, it was well said, *Pompa mortis magis terret quam mors ipsa.* Groans and convulsions, and a discoloured face, and friends weeping, and blacks, and obsequies, and the like, shew death terrible. It is worthy the observing, that there is no passion in the mind of man so weak, but it mates and masters the fear of death; and therefore death is no such terrible enemy, when a man hath so many attendants about him that can win the combat of him. Revenge triumphs over death; love slights it; honour aspireth to it; grief flieth to it; fear pre-occupateth it; nay, we read, after Otho the emperor had slain himself, pity (which is the tenderest of affections) provoked many to die, out of mere compassion to their sovereign, and as the truest sort of followers. Nay, Seneca adds niceness and satiety: *Cogita quam diu eadem feceris ; mori velle, non tantum fortis, aut miser, sed etiam fastidiosus potest.* A

Of Death

man would die, though he were neither valiant nor miserable, only upon a weariness to do the same thing so oft over and over. It is no less worthy to observe, how little alteration, in good spirits, the approaches of death make; for they appear to be the same men till the last instant. Augustus Cæsar died in a compliment: *Livia, conjugii nostri memor, vive et vale.* Tiberius in dissimulation, as Tacitus saith of him: *Jam Tiberium vires et corpus, non dissimulatio, deserebant.* Vespasian in a jest, sitting upon the stool: *Ut puto Deus fio.* Galba with a sentence, *Feri, si ex re sit populi Romani,* holding forth his neck. Septimius Severus in dispatch: *Adeste si quid mihi restat agendum.* And the like. Certainly the Stoics bestowed too much cost upon death, and by their great preparations made it appear more fearful. Better saith he, *Qui finem vitæ extremum inter munera ponat Naturæ.* It is as natural to die as to be born; and to a little infant, perhaps, the one is as painful as the other. He that dies in an earnest pursuit is like one that is wounded in hot blood; who, for the time, scarce feels the hurt; and therefore a mind fixed and bent upon somewhat that is good doth avert the dolours of death. But above all, believe it, the sweetest canticle is *Nunc dimittis;* when a man hath obtained worthy ends and expectations. Death hath this also, that it openeth the gate to good fame, and extinguisheth envy.—*Extinctus amabitur idem.*

Essay III.—OF UNITY IN RELIGION

Religion being the chief band of human society, it is a happy thing when itself is well contained within the true band of unity. The quarrels and divisions about religions were evils unknown to the heathen. The reason was, because the religion of the heathen consisted rather in rites and ceremonies, than in any constant belief. For you may imagine what kind of faith theirs was, when the chief doctors and fathers of their church were the poets. But the true God hath this attribute, that he is a *jealous God ;* and therefore his worship and religion will endure no mixture nor partner. We shall therefore speak a few words concerning the unity of the church; what are the fruits thereof; what the bounds; and what the means.

The fruits of unity (next unto the well pleasing of God, which is all in all) are two; the one towards those that are without the church, the other towards those that are within. For the former; it is certain that heresies and schisms are of all others the greatest scandals; yea, more than corruption of manners. For as in the natural body a wound or solution of continuity is worse than a corrupt humour, so in the spiritual. So that nothing doth so much keep men out of the church, and drive men out of the church, as breach of unity. And therefore, whensoever it cometh to that pass, that one saith *Ecce in deserto,* another saith *Ecce in penetralibus ;* that is, when some men seek Christ in the conventicles of heretics, and others in an outward face of a church, that voice had need continually to sound in men's ears, *Nolite exire,—Go not out.* The doctor of the Gentiles (the propriety of whose vocation drew him to have a special care of those without) saith, *If an*

8

Of Unity in Religion

heathen come in, and hear you speak with several tongues, will he not say that you are mad? And certainly it is little better, when atheists and profane persons do hear of so many discordant and contrary opinions in religion; it doth avert them from the church, and maketh them *to sit down in the chair of the scorners.* It is but a light thing to be vouched in so serious a matter, but yet it expresseth well the deformity. There is a master of scoffing, that in his catalogue of books of a feigned library sets down this title of a book, *The morris dance of heretics.* For indeed every sect of them hath a diverse posture or cringe by themselves, which cannot but move derision in worldlings and depraved politics, who are apt to contemn holy things.

As for the fruit towards those that are within, it is peace, which containeth infinite blessings: it establisheth faith; it kindleth charity; the outward peace of the church distilleth into peace of conscience; and it turneth the labours of writing and reading of controversies into treaties of mortification and devotion.

Concerning the bounds of unity; the true placing of them importeth exceedingly. There appear to be two extremes. For to certain zelants all speech of pacification is odious. *Is it peace, Jehu? What hast thou to do with peace? turn thee behind me.* Peace is not the matter, but following and party. Contrariwise, certain Laodiceans and lukewarm persons think they may accommodate points of religion by middle ways, and taking part of both, and witty reconcilements; as if they would make an arbitrement between God and man. Both these extremes are to be avoided; which will be done, if the league of Christians penned by our Saviour Himself were in the two cross clauses thereof soundly and plainly expounded: *He that is not with us is against us;* and again, *He that is not against us is with us:* that is, if the points fundamental and of substance in religion were truly discerned and distinguished from points not merely of faith, but of opinion, order, or good intention. This is a thing may seem to many a matter trivial and done already; but if it were done less partially, it would be embraced more generally.

Of this I may give only this advice, according to my small model. Men ought to take heed of rending God's church by two kinds of controversies. The one is, when the matter of the point controverted is too small and light, not worth the heat and strife about it, kindled only by contradiction. For, as it is noted by one of the fathers, *Christ's coat indeed had no seam, but the church's vesture was of divers colours;* whereupon he saith, *In veste varietas sit, scissura non sit:* they be two things, unity and uniformity. The other is, when the matter of the point controverted is great, but it is driven to an over-great subtilty and obscurity; so that it becometh a thing rather ingenious than substantial. A man that is of judgement and understanding shall sometimes hear ignorant men differ, and know well within himself that those which so differ mean one thing, and yet they themselves would never agree. And if it come so to pass in that distance of judgement which is between man and man, shall we not think that God above, that knows the heart, doth not discern that frail men in some of their contradictions intend the same thing, and accepteth of both? The nature of such controversies is excellently expressed by St. Paul in the warning and precept that he giveth concerning the same, *Devita profanas vocum novitates, et oppositiones falsi nominis scientiæ.* Men create oppositions which are not; and put them into new terms so fixed, as whereas the meaning ought to govern the term, the term in effect governeth the meaning. There be also two false peaces or unities: the one, when the peace is grounded but upon an implicit ignorance; for all colours will agree in the dark: the other, when it is pieced up upon a direct admission of contraries in fundamental points. For truth and falsehood, in such things, are like the iron and clay in the toes of Nebuchadnezzar's image; they may cleave, but they will not incorporate.

Concerning the means of procuring unity; men must beware, that in the procuring or muniting of religious unity, they do not dissolve and deface the laws of charity and of human society. There be two swords amongst Christians, the spiritual and temporal; and both have their due office and place in the maintenance of religion. But we may not take up the third sword, which is Mahomet's sword, or like unto it; that is, to propagate religion by wars, or by sanguinary persecutions to force consciences; except it be in cases of overt scandal, blasphemy, or intermixture of practice against the state; much less to nourish seditions; to authorize conspiracies and rebellions; to put the sword into the people's hands; and the like; tending to the subversion of all government, which is the ordinance of God. For this is but to dash the first table against the second; and so to consider men as Christians, as we forget that they are men. Lucretius the poet, when he beheld the act of Agamemnon, that could endure the sacrificing of his own daughter, exclaimed:

Tantum religio potuit suadere malorum.

What would he have said, if he had known of the massacre in France, or the powder treason of England? He would have been seven times more Epicure and atheist than he was. For as the temporal sword is to be drawn with great circumspection in cases of religion; so it is a thing monstrous to put it into the hands of the common people. Let that be left unto the Anabaptists, and other furies. It was great blasphemy when the devil said, *I will ascend and be like the Highest;* but it is greater blasphemy to personate God, and bring him in saying, *I will descend and be like the prince of darkness:* and what is it better, to make the cause of religion to descend to the cruel and execrable actions of murthering princes, butchery of people, and subversion of states and governments? Surely this is to bring down the Holy Ghost, in stead of the likeness of a dove, in the shape of a vulture or raven; and to set out of the bark of a Christian church a flag of a bark of pirates and assassins. Therefore it is most necessary that the church by doctrine and decree, princes by their

Essay IV.—OF REVENGE

REVENGE is a kind of wild justice; which the more man's nature runs to, the more ought law to weed it out. For as for the first wrong, it doth but offend the law; but the revenge of that wrong putteth the law out of office. Certainly, in taking revenge, a man is but even with his enemy; but in passing it over, he is superior; for it is a prince's part to pardon. And Salomon, I am sure, saith, *It is the glory of a man to pass by an offence.* That which is past is gone, and irrevocable; and wise men have enough to do with things present and to come: therefore they do but trifle with themselves, that labour in past matters. There is no man doth a wrong for the wrong's sake; but thereby to purchase himself profit, or pleasure, or honour, or the like. Therefore why should I be angry with a man for loving himself better than me? And if any man should do wrong merely out of ill nature, why, yet it is but like the thorn or briar, which prick and scratch, because they can do no other. The most tolerable sort of revenge is for those wrongs which there is no law to remedy; but then let a man take heed the revenge be such as there is no law to punish; else a man's enemy is still beforehand, and it is two for one. Some, when they take revenge, are desirous the party should know whence it cometh: this is the more generous. For the delight seemeth to be not so much in doing the hurt as in making the party repent: but base and crafty cowards are like the arrow that flieth in the dark. Cosmus, duke of Florence, had a desperate saying against perfidious or neglecting friends, as if those wrongs were unpardonable: *You shall read* (saith he) *that we are commanded to forgive our enemies; but you never read that we are commanded to forgive our friends.* But yet the spirit of Job was in a better tune: *Shall we* (saith he) *take good*

13

at God's hands, and not be content to take evil also?
And so of friends in a proportion. This is certain, that
a man that studieth revenge keeps his own wounds
green, which otherwise would heal and do well. Public
revenges are for the most part fortunate; as that for the
death of Cæsar; for the death of Pertinax; for the
death of Henry the Third of France; and many more.
But in private revenges it is not so. Nay rather, vindicative persons live the life of witches; who as they are
mischievous, so end they infortunate.

Essay V.—OF ADVERSITY

IT was an high speech of Seneca (after the manner of
the Stoics): *That the good things which belong to prosperity are to be wished ; but the good things that belong to
adversity are to be admired. Bona rerum secundarum
optabilia, adversarum mirabilia.* Certainly, if miracles
be the command over nature, they appear most in
adversity. It is yet a higher speech of his than the
other (much too high for a heathen): *It is true greatness
to have in one the frailty of a man, and the security of a
god. Vere magnum, habere fragilitatem hominis, securi-
tatem dei.* This would have done better in poesy,
where transcendences are more allowed. And the poets
indeed have been busy with it; for it is in effect the
thing which is figured in that strange fiction of the
ancient poets, which seemeth not to be without mystery;
nay, and to have some approach to the state of a
Christian: that *Hercules, when he went to unbind
Prometheus* (by whom human nature is represented),
*sailed the length of the great ocean in an earthen pot or
pitcher:* lively describing Christian resolution, that
saileth in the frail bark of the flesh thorough the waves
of the world. But to speak in a mean. The virtue of
prosperity is temperance; the virtue of adversity is
fortitude; which in morals is the more heroical virtue.
Prosperity is the blessing of the Old Testament; adversity is the blessing of the New; which carrieth the
greater benediction, and the clearer revelation of God's
favour. Yet even in the Old Testament, if you listen
to David's harp, you shall hear as many hearse-like airs
as carols; and the pencil of the Holy Ghost hath
laboured more in describing the afflictions of Job than
the felicities of Salomon. Prosperity is not without
many fears and distastes; and adversity is not without
comforts and hopes. We see in needleworks and

15

embroideries, it is more pleasing to have a lively work upon a sad and solemn ground, than to have a dark and melancholy work upon a lightsome ground: judge therefore of the pleasure of the heart by the pleasure of the eye. Certainly virtue is like precious odours, most fragrant when they are incensed or crushed: for prosperity doth best discover vice; but adversity doth best discover virtue.

Essay VI.—OF SIMULATION AND DISSIMULATION

DISSIMULATION is but a faint kind of policy or wisdom; for it asketh a strong wit and a strong heart to know when to tell truth, and to do it. Therefore it is the weaker sort of politics that are the great dissemblers.

Tacitus saith, *Livia sorted well with the arts of her husband and dissimulation of her son;* attributing arts or policy to Augustus, and dissimulation to Tiberius. And again, when Mucianus encourageth Vespasian to take arms against Vitellius, he saith, *We rise not against the piercing judgement of Augustus, nor the extreme caution or closeness of Tiberius.* These properties, of arts or policy, and dissimulation or closeness, are indeed habits and faculties several and to be distinguished. For if a man have that penetration of judgement as he can discern what things are to be laid open, and what to be secreted, and what to be shewed at half lights, and to whom, and when (which indeed are arts of state and arts of life, as Tacitus well calleth them), to him a habit of dissimulation is a hinderance and a poorness. But if a man cannot obtain to that judgement, then it is left to him, generally, to be close, and a dissembler. For where a man cannot choose or vary in particulars, there it is good to take the safest and wariest way in general; like the going softly by one that cannot well see. Certainly the ablest men that ever were have had all an openness and frankness of dealing, and a name of certainty and veracity; but then they were like horses well managed; for they could tell passing well when to stop or turn; and at such times when they thought the case indeed required dissimulation, if then they used it, it came to pass that the former opinion spread abroad of their good faith and clearness of dealing made them almost invisible.

There be three degrees of this hiding and veiling of

a man's self. The first, closeness, reservation, and secrecy; when a man leaveth himself without observation, or without hold to be taken, what he is. The second, dissimulation, in the negative; when a man lets fall signs and arguments, that he is not that he is. And the third, simulation, in the affirmative; when a man industriously and expressly feigns and pretends to be that he is not.

For the first of these, secrecy: it is indeed the virtue of a confessor; and assuredly the secret man heareth many confessions; for who will open himself to a blab or a babbler? But if a man be thought secret, it inviteth discovery; as the more close air sucketh in the more open: and as in confession the revealing is not for worldly use, but for the ease of a man's heart, so secret men come to the knowledge of many things in that kind; while men rather discharge their minds than impart their minds. In few words, mysteries are due to secrecy. Besides (to say truth) nakedness is uncomely, as well in mind as body; and it addeth no small reverence to men's manners and actions, if they be not altogether open. As for talkers and futile persons, they are commonly vain and credulous withal. For he that talketh what he knoweth, will also talk what he knoweth not. Therefore set it down, *that an habit of secrecy is both politic and moral.* And in this part, it is good that a man's face give his tongue leave to speak. For the discovery of a man's self by the tracts of his countenance is a great weakness and betraying; by how much it is many times more marked and believed than a man's words.

For the second, which is dissimulation: it followeth many times upon secrecy by a necessity; so that he that will be secret must be a dissembler in some degree. For men are too cunning to suffer a man to keep an indifferent carriage between both, and to be secret, without swaying the balance on either side. They will so beset a man with questions, and draw him on, and pick it out of him, that, without an absurd silence, he must shew an inclination one way; or if he do not, they will gather as much by his silence as by his speech. As for equivoca-

Of Simulation and Dissimulation

tions, or oraculous speeches, they cannot hold out long. So that no man can be secret, except he give himself a little scope of dissimulation; which is, as it were, but the skirts or train of secrecy.

But for the third degree, which is simulation and false profession: that I hold more culpable, and less politic; except it be in great and rare matters. And therefore a general custom of simulation (which is this last degree) is a vice, rising either of a natural falseness or fearfulness, or of a mind that hath some main faults, which because a man must needs disguise, it maketh him practise simulation in other things, lest his hand should be out of use.

The great advantages of simulation and dissimulation are three. First, to lay asleep opposition, and to surprise. For where a man's intentions are published, it is an alarum to call up all that are against them. The second is, to reserve to a man's self a fair retreat. For if a man engage himself by a manifest declaration, he must go through, or take a fall. The third is, the better to discover the mind of another. For to him that opens himself men will hardly shew themselves adverse; but will (fair) let him go on, and turn their freedom of speech to freedom of thought. And therefore it is a good shrewd proverb of the Spaniard, *Tell a lie and find a troth ;* as if there were no way of discovery but by simulation. There be also three disadvantages, to set it even. The first, that simulation and dissimulation commonly carry with them a shew of fearfulness, which in any business doth spoil the feathers of round flying up to the mark. The second, that it puzzleth and perplexeth the conceits of many that perhaps would otherwise co-operate with him, and makes a man walk almost alone to his own ends. The third and greatest is, that it depriveth a man of one of the most principal instruments for action, which is trust and belief. The best composition and temperature is to have openness in fame and opinion; secrecy in habit; dissimulation in seasonable use; and a power to feign, if there be no remedy.

Essay VII.—OF PARENTS AND CHILDREN

THE joys of parents are secret, and so are their griefs and fears: they cannot utter the one, nor they will not utter the other. Children sweeten labours, but they make misfortunes more bitter: they increase the cares of life, but they mitigate the remembrance of death. The perpetuity by generation is common to beasts; but memory, merit, and noble works are proper to men: and surely a man shall see the noblest works and foundations have proceeded from childless men, which have sought to express the images of their minds, where those of their bodies have failed: so the care of posterity is most in them that have no posterity. They that are the first raisers of their houses are most indulgent towards their children; beholding them as the continuance not only of their kind but of their work; and so both children and creatures.

The difference in affection of parents towards their several children is many times unequal, and sometimes unworthy, especially in the mother; as Salomon saith, *A wise son rejoiceth the father, but an ungracious son shames the mother.* A man shall see, where there is a house full of children, one or two of the eldest respected, and the youngest made wantons; but in the midst some that are as it were forgotten, who many times nevertheless prove the best. The illiberality of parents in allowance towards their children is an harmful error; makes them base; acquaints them with shifts; makes them sort with mean company; and makes them surfeit more when they come to plenty: and therefore the proof is best, when men keep their authority towards their children, but not their purse. Men have a foolish manner (both parents and schoolmasters and servants)

Of Parents and Children

in creating and breeding an emulation between brothers during childhood, which many times sorteth to discord when they are men, and disturbeth families. The Italians make little difference between children and nephews or near kinsfolks; but so they be of the lump, they care not though they pass not through their own body. And, to say truth, in nature it is much a like matter; insomuch that we see a nephew sometimes resembleth an uncle or a kinsman more than his own parent; as the blood happens. Let parents choose betimes the vocations and courses they mean their children should take; for then they are most flexible; and let them not too much apply themselves to the disposition of their children, as thinking they will take best to that which they have most mind to. It is true, that if the affection or aptness of the children be extra-ordinary, then it is good not to cross it; but generally the precept is good, *Optimum elige, suave et facile illud faciet consuetudo*. Younger brothers are commonly fortunate, but seldom or never where the elder are disinherited.

Essay VIII.—OF MARRIAGE AND SINGLE LIFE

He that hath wife and children hath given hostages to fortune; for they are impediments to great enterprises, either of virtue or mischief. Certainly, the best works, and of greatest merit for the public, have proceeded from the unmarried or childless men, which both in affection and means have married and endowed the public. Yet it were great reason that those that have children should have greatest care of future times; unto which they know they must transmit their dearest pledges. Some there are, who though they lead a single life, yet their thoughts do end with themselves, and account future times impertinences. Nay, there are some other that account wife and children but as bills of charges. Nay more, there are some foolish rich covetous men that take a pride in having no children, because they may be thought so much the richer. For perhaps they have heard some talk, *Such an one is a great rich man,* and another except to it, *Yea, but he hath a great charge of children ;* as if it were an abatement to his riches. But the most ordinary cause of a single life is liberty; especially in certain self-pleasing and humorous minds, which are so sensible of every restraint, as they will go near to think their girdles and garters to be bonds and shackles. Unmarried men are best friends, best masters, best servants; but not always best subjects; for they are light to run away; and almost all fugitives are of that condition. A single life doth well with churchmen; for charity will hardly water the ground where it must first fill a pool. It is indifferent for judges and magistrates; for if they be facile and corrupt, you shall have a servant five times worse than a wife. For soldiers, I find the generals commonly in their

22

Of Marriage and Single Life

hortatives put men in mind of their wives and children; and I think the despising of marriage amongst the Turks maketh the vulgar soldier more base. Certainly wife and children are a kind of discipline of humanity; and single men, though they be many times more charitable, because their means are less exhaust, yet, on the other side, they are more cruel and hard-hearted (good to make severe inquisitors), because their tenderness is not so oft called upon. Grave natures, led by custom, and therefore constant, are commonly loving husbands; as was said of Ulysses, *Vetulam suam prætulit immortalitati*. Chaste women are often proud and froward, as presuming upon the merit of their chastity. It is one of the best bonds both of chastity and obedience in the wife, if she think her husband wise; which she will never do if she find him jealous. Wives are young men's mistresses; companions for middle age; and old men's nurses. So as a man may have a quarrel to marry when he will. But yet he was reputed one of the wise men, that made answer to the question, when a man should marry? *A young man not yet, an elder man not at all*. It is often seen that bad husbands have very good wives; whether it be that it raiseth the price of their husband's kindness when it comes; or that the wives take a pride in their patience. But this never fails, if the bad husbands were of their own choosing, against their friends' consent; for then they will be sure to make good their own folly.

Essay IX.—OF ENVY

THERE be none of the affections which have been noted to fascinate or bewitch, but love and envy. They both have vehement wishes; they frame themselves readily into imaginations and suggestions; and they come easily into the eye, especially upon the presence of the objects; which are the points that conduce to fascination, if any such thing there be. We see, likewise, the scripture calleth envy an *evil eye;* and the astrologers call the evil influences of the stars *evil aspects;* so that still there seemeth to be acknowledged, in the act of envy, an ejaculation or irradiation of the eye. Nay, some have been so curious as to note, that the times when the stroke or percussion of an envious eye doth most hurt, are when the party envied is beheld in glory or triumph; for that sets an edge upon envy; and besides, at such times the spirits of the person envied do come forth most into the outward parts, and so meet the blow.

But leaving these curiosities (though not unworthy to be thought on in fit place), we will handle, what persons are apt to envy others; what persons are most subject to be envied themselves; and what is the difference between public and private envy.

A man that hath no virtue in himself ever envieth virtue in others. For men's minds will either feed upon their own good, or upon others' evil; and who wanteth the one will prey upon the other; and whoso is out of hope to attain to another's virtue will seek to come at even hand by depressing another's fortune.

A man that is busy and inquisitive is commonly envious. For to know much of other men's matters cannot be because all that ado may concern his own estate; therefore it must needs be that he taketh a kind of play-pleasure in looking upon the fortunes of others. Neither can he that mindeth but his own business find

24

Of Envy

much matter for envy. For envy is a gadding passion, and walketh the streets, and doth not keep home: *Non est curiosus, quin idem sit malevolus.*

Men of noble birth are noted to be envious towards new men when they rise. For the distance is altered; and it is like a deceit of the eye, that when others come on they think themselves go back.

Deformed persons, and eunuchs, and old men, and bastards, are envious. For he that cannot possibly mend his own case, will do what he can to impair another's. Except these defects light upon a very brave and heroical nature, which thinketh to make his natural wants part of his honour; in that it should be said, that an eunuch, or a lame man, did such great matters; affecting the honour of a miracle; as it was in Narses the eunuch, and Agesilaus and Tamberlanes, that were lame men.

The same is the case of men that rise after calamities and misfortunes. For they are as men fallen out with the times, and think other men's harms a redemption of their own sufferings.

They that desire to excel in too many matters, out of levity and vain glory, are ever envious. For they cannot want work; it being impossible but many in some one of those things should surpass them. Which was the character of Adrian the Emperor, that mortally envied poets and painters and artificers in works wherein he had a vein to excel.

Lastly, near kinsfolks, and fellows in office, and those that have been bred together, are more apt to envy their equals when they are raised. For it doth upbraid unto them their own fortunes, and pointeth at them, and cometh oftener into their remembrance, and incurreth likewise more into the note of others; and envy ever redoubleth from speech and fame. Cain's envy was the more vile and malignant towards his brother Abel, because when his sacrifice was better accepted there was nobody to look on. Thus much for those that are apt to envy.

Concerning those that are more or less subject to envy. First, persons of eminent virtue, when they are advanced, are less envied. For their fortune seemeth but due unto them; and no man envieth the payment of a debt, but rewards and liberality rather. Again, envy is ever joined with the comparing of a man's self; and where there is no comparison, no envy; and therefore kings are not envied but by kings. Nevertheless it is to be noted that unworthy persons are most envied at their first coming in, and afterwards overcome it better; whereas, contrariwise, persons of worth and merit are most envied when their fortune continueth long. For by that time, though their virtue be the same, yet it hath not the same lustre; for fresh men grow up that darken it.

Persons of noble blood are less envied in their rising; for it seemeth but right done to their birth. Besides, there seemeth not much added to their fortune; and envy is as the sunbeams, that beat hotter upon a bank or steep rising ground, than upon a flat. And for the same reason those that are advanced by degrees are less envied than those that are advanced suddenly and *per saltum*.

Those that have joined with their honour great travails, cares, or perils, are less subject to envy. For men think that they earn their honours hardly, and pity them sometimes; and pity ever healeth envy. Wherefore you shall observe that the more deep and sober sort of politic persons, in their greatness, are ever bemoaning themselves, what a life they lead; chanting a *quanta patimur*. Not that they feel it so, but only to abate the edge of envy. But this is to be understood of business that is laid upon men, and not such as they call unto themselves. For nothing increaseth envy more than an unnecessary and ambitious engrossing of business. And nothing doth extinguish envy more than for a great person to preserve all other inferior officers in their full rights and pre-eminences of their places. For by that means there be so many screens between him and envy.

Above all, those are most subject to envy, which carry the greatness of their fortunes in an insolent and

Of Envy

proud manner; being never well but while they are shewing how great they are, either by outward pomp, or by triumphing over all opposition or competition; whereas wise men will rather do sacrifice to envy, in suffering themselves sometimes of purpose to be crossed and overborne in things that do not much concern them. Notwithstanding, so much is true, that the carriage of greatness in a plain and open manner (so it be without arrogancy and vain-glory) doth draw less envy than if it be in a more crafty and cunning fashion. For in that course a man doth but disavow fortune; and seemeth to be conscious of his own want in worth; and doth but teach others to envy him.

Lastly, to conclude this part; as we said in the beginning that the act of envy had somewhat in it of witchcraft, so there is no other cure of envy but the cure of witchcraft; and that is, to remove the *lot* (as they call it) and to lay it upon another. For which purpose the wiser sort of great persons bring in ever upon the stage somebody upon whom to derive the envy that would come upon themselves; sometimes upon ministers and servants; sometimes upon colleagues and associates; and the like; and for that turn there are never wanting some persons of violent and under-taking natures, who, so they may have power and busi-ness, will take it at any cost.

Now to speak of public envy. There is yet some good in public envy, whereas in private there is none. For public envy is as an ostracism, that eclipseth men when they grow too great. And therefore it is a bridle also to great ones, to keep them within bounds.

This envy, being in the Latin word *invidia*, goeth in the modern languages by the name of *discontentment :* of which we shall speak in handling Sedition. It is a disease in a state like to infection. For as infection spreadeth upon that which is sound, and tainteth it; so when envy is gotten once into a state, it traduceth even the best actions thereof, and turneth them into an ill odour. And therefore there is little won by intermingl-ing of plausible actions. For that doth argue but a weakness and fear of envy, which hurteth so much the more; as it is likewise usual in infections; which if you fear them, you call them upon you.

This public envy seemeth to beat chiefly upon principal officers or ministers, rather than upon kings and estates themselves. But this is a sure rule, that if the envy upon the ministers be great, when the cause of it in him is small; or if the envy be general in a manner upon all the ministers of an estate; then the envy (though hidden) is truly upon the estate itself. And so much of public envy or discontentment, and the difference thereof from private envy, which was handled in the first place.

We will add this, in general, touching the affection of envy, that of all other affections it is the most importune and continual. For of other affections there is occasion given but now and then. And therefore it was well said, *Invidia festos dies non agit.* For it is ever working upon some or other. And it is also noted that love and envy do make a man pine, which other affections do not, because they are not so continual. It is also the vilest affection, and the most depraved; for which cause it is the proper attribute of the devil, who is called *The envious man, that soweth tares amongst the wheat by night :* as it always cometh to pass, that envy worketh subtilly, and in the dark, and to the prejudice of good things, such as is the wheat.

Essay X.—OF LOVE

THE stage is more beholding to love than the life of man. For as to the stage, love is ever matter of comedies, and now and then of tragedies: but in life it doth much mischief; sometimes like a siren, sometimes like a fury. You may observe, that amongst all the great and worthy persons (whereof the memory remaineth, either ancient or recent), there is not one that hath been transported to the mad degree of love; which shows that great spirits and great business do keep out this weak passion. You must except, nevertheless, Marcus Antonius, the half partner of the empire of Rome, and Appius Claudius, the decemvir and lawgiver: whereof the former was indeed a voluptuous man, and inordinate; but the latter was an austere and wise man: and therefore it seems (though rarely) that love can find entrance not only into an open heart, but also into a heart well fortified, if watch be not well kept. It is a poor saying of Epicurus, *Satis magnum alter alteri theatrum sumus:* as if man, made for the contemplation of heaven and all noble objects, should do nothing but kneel before a little idol, and make himself subject, though not of the mouth (as beasts are), yet of the eye, which was given them for higher purposes. It is a strange thing to note the excess of this passion, and how it braves the nature and value of things, by this, that the speaking in a perpetual hyperbole is comely in nothing but in love. Neither is it merely in the phrase; for whereas it hath been well said that the arch-flatterer, with whom all the petty flatterers have intelligence, is a man's self, certainly the lover is more. For there was never proud man thought so absurdly well of himself as the lover doth of the person loved: and therefore it was well said, *That it is impossible to love and to be wise.* Neither doth this weakness appear to others only, and not to the party loved, but to the loved most of all, except the love be reciproque. For it is a true rule, that love is ever rewarded either with the reciproque or with an inward and secret contempt. By how much the more men ought to beware of this passion, which loseth not only other things, but itself. As for the other losses, the poet's relation doth well figure them: That he that preferred Helena, quitted the gifts of Juno and Pallas. For whosoever esteemeth too much of amorous affection, quitteth both riches and wisdom. This passion hath his floods in the very times of weakness; which are great prosperity and great adversity (though this latter hath been less observed): both which times kindle love, and make it more fervent, and therefore show it to be the child of folly. They do best, who, if they cannot but admit love, yet make it keep quarter, and sever it wholly from their serious affairs and actions of life; for if it check once with business, it troubleth men's fortunes, and maketh men that they can no ways be true to their own ends. I know not how, but martial men are given to love: I think it is but as they are given to wine; for perils commonly ask to be paid in pleasures. There is in man's nature a secret inclination and motion towards love of others, which, if it be not spent upon some one or a few, doth naturally spread itself towards many, and maketh men become humane and charitable; as it is seen sometime in friars. Nuptial love maketh mankind; friendly love perfecteth it; but wanton love corrupteth and embaseth it.

(though God accept them) yet towards men are little better than good dreams, except they be put in act; and that cannot be without power and place, as the vantage and commanding ground. Merit and good works is the end of man's motion; and conscience of the same is the accomplishment of man's rest. For if a man can be partaker of God's theatre, he shall likewise be partaker of God's rest. *Et conversus Deus, ut aspiceret opera quæ fecerunt manus suæ, vidit quod omnia essent bona nimis;* and then the Sabbath. In the discharge of thy place, set before thee the best examples; for imitation is a globe of precepts. And after a time set before thee thine own example; and examine thyself strictly, whether thou didst not best at first. Neglect not also the examples of those that have carried themselves ill in the same place; not to set off thyself by taxing their memory, but to direct thyself what to avoid. Reform, therefore, without bravery or scandal of former times and persons; but yet set it down to thyself as well to create good precedents as to follow them. Reduce things to the first institution, and observe wherein and how they have degenerate; but yet ask counsel of both times; of the ancient time, what is best; and of the latter time, what is fittest. Seek to make thy course regular, that men may know beforehand what they may expect; but be not too positive and peremptory; and express thyself well when thou digressest from thy rule. Preserve the right of thy place, but stir not questions of jurisdiction: and rather assume thy right in silence and *de facto*, than voice it with claims and challenges. Preserve likewise the rights of inferior places; and think it more honour to direct in chief than to be busy in all. Embrace and invite helps and advices touching the execution of thy place; and do not drive away such as bring thee information as meddlers, but accept of them in good part. The vices of authority are chiefly four: delays, corruption, roughness, and facility. For delays; give easy access; keep times appointed; go through with that which is in hand; and interlace not business but of necessity. For corruption; do not

Of Great Place

only bind thine own hands or thy servants' hands from taking, but bind the hands of suitors also from offering. For integrity used doth the one; but integrity professed, and with a manifest detestation of bribery, doth the other. And avoid not only the fault, but the suspicion. Whosoever is found variable, and changeth manifestly without manifest cause, giveth suspicion of corruption. Therefore always when thou changest thine opinion or course, profess it plainly and declare it, together with the reasons that move thee to change; and do not think to steal it. A servant or a favourite, if he be inward, and no other apparent cause of esteem, is commonly thought but a by-way to close corruption. For roughness, it is a needless cause of discontent: severity breedeth fear, but roughness breedeth hate. Even reproofs from authority ought to be grave, and not taunting. As for facility, it is worse than bribery. For bribes come but now and then; but if importunity or idle respects lead a man, he shall never be without. As Salomon saith: *To respect persons is not good ; for such a man will transgress for a piece of bread.* It is most true that was anciently spoken, *A place sheweth the man :* and it sheweth some to the better, and some to the worse. *Omnium consensu capax imperii, nisi imperasset*, saith Tacitus of Galba; but of Vespasian he saith, *Solus imperantium Vespasianus mutatus in melius :* though the one was meant of sufficiency, the other of manners and affection. It is an assured sign of a worthy and generous spirit, whom honour amends. For honour is, or should be, the place of virtue; and as in nature things move violently to their place, and calmly in their place; so virtue in ambition is violent, in authority settled and calm. All rising to great place is by a winding stair; and if there be factions, it is good to side a man's self whilst he is in the rising, and to balance himself when he is placed. Use the memory of thy predecessor fairly and tenderly; for if thou dost not, it is a debt will sure be paid when thou art gone. If thou have colleagues, respect them, and rather call them when they look not for it, than exclude them

Essay XII.—OF BOLDNESS

It is a trivial grammar-school text, but yet worthy a wise man's consideration. Question was asked of Demosthenes, *what was the chief part of an orator?* he answered, *action :* what next? *action :* what next again? *action.* He said it that knew it best, and had by nature himself no advantage in that he commended. A strange thing, that that part of an orator which is but superficial, and rather the virtue of a player, should be placed so high above those other noble parts of invention, elocution, and the rest; nay, almost alone, as if it were all in all. But the reason is plain. There is in human nature generally more of the fool than of the wise; and therefore those faculties by which the foolish part of men's minds is taken are most potent. Wonderful like is the case of boldness in civil business: what first? *boldness :* what second and third? *boldness.* And yet boldness is a child of ignorance and baseness, far inferior to other parts. But nevertheless it doth fascinate and bind hand and foot those that are either shallow in judgement or weak in courage, which are the greatest part; yea, and prevaileth with wise men at weak times. Therefore we see it hath done wonders in popular states, but with senates and princes less; and more ever upon the first entrance of bold persons into action than soon after; for boldness is an ill keeper of promise. Surely, as there are mountebanks for the natural body, so are there mountebanks for the politic body; men that undertake great cures, and perhaps have been lucky in two or three experiments, but want the grounds of science, and therefore cannot hold out. Nay, you shall see a bold fellow many times do Mahomet's miracle. Mahomet made the people believe that he would call an hill to him, and from the top of it offer up his prayers for the observers of his law. The people assembled; Mahomet called the hill to come to him, again and again; and when the hill stood still, he was never a whit abashed, but said, *If the hill will not come to Mahomet, Mahomet will go to the hill.* So these men, when they have promised great matters and failed most shamefully, yet (if they have the perfection of boldness) they will but slight it over, and make a turn, and no more ado. Certainly, to men of great judgement, bold persons are a sport to behold; nay, and to the vulgar also, boldness hath somewhat of the ridiculous. For if absurdity be the subject of laughter, doubt you not but great boldness is seldom without some absurdity. Especially it is a sport to see, when a bold fellow is out of countenance; for that puts his face into a most shrunken and wooden posture; as needs it must; for in bashfulness the spirits do a little go and come; but with bold men, upon like occasion, they stand at a stay; like a stale at chess, where it is no mate, but yet the game cannot stir. But this last were fitter for a satire than for a serious observation. This is well to be weighed, that boldness is ever blind; for it seeth not dangers and inconveniences. Therefore it is ill in counsel, good in execution; so that the right use of bold persons is, that they never command in chief, but be seconds, and under the direction of others. For in counsel it is good to see dangers; and in execution not to see them, except they be very great.

habit so excellent. Seek the good of other men, but be not in bondage to their faces or fancies; for that is but facility or softness; which taketh an honest mind prisoner. Neither give thou Æsop's cock a gem, who would be better pleased and happier if he had had a barley-corn. The example of God teacheth the lesson truly: *He sendeth his rain, and maketh his sun to shine, upon the just and unjust ;* but he doth not rain wealth, nor shine honour and virtues, upon men equally. Common benefits are to be communicate with all, but peculiar benefits with choice. And beware how in making the portraiture thou breakest the pattern; for divinity maketh the love of ourselves the pattern, the love of our neighbours but the portraiture. *Sell all thou hast, and give it to the poor, and follow me* : but sell not all thou hast, except thou come and follow me; that is, except thou have a vocation wherein thou mayest do as much good with little means as with great; for otherwise in feeding the streams thou driest the fountain. Neither is there only a habit of goodness, directed by right reason; but there is in some men, even in nature, a disposition towards it; as on the other side there is a natural malignity. For there be that in their nature do not affect the good of others. The lighter sort of malignity turneth but to a crossness, or frowardness, or aptness to oppose, or difficilness, or the like; but the deeper sort, to envy and mere mischief. Such men in other men's calamities are, as it were, in season, and are ever on the loading part; not so good as the dogs that licked Lazarus' sores, but like flies that are still buzzing upon anything that is raw; *misanthropi*, that make it their practice to bring men to the bough, and yet have never a tree for the purpose in their gardens, as Timon had. Such dispositions are the very errors of human nature; and yet they are the fittest timber to make great politics of; like to knee-timber, that is good for ships that are ordained to be tossed, but not for building houses that shall stand firm. The parts and signs of goodness are many. If a man be gracious and courteous to strangers, it shews he is a citizen of the

Of Goodness, Etc.

world, and that his heart is no island cut off from other lands, but a continent that joins to them. If he be compassionate towards the afflictions of others, it shews that his heart is like the noble tree, that is wounded itself when it gives the balm. If he easily pardons and remits offences, it shews that his mind is planted above injuries, so that he cannot be shot. If he be thankful for small benefits, it shews that he weighs men's minds, and not their trash. But above all, if he have St. Paul's perfection, that he would wish to be an *anathema* from Christ for the salvation of his brethren, it shews much of a divine nature, and a kind of conformity with Christ Himself.

Essay XIV.—OF NOBILITY

WE will speak of nobility first as a portion of an estate; then as a condition of particular persons. A monarchy where there is no nobility at all, is ever a pure and absolute tyranny; as that of the Turks. For nobility attempers sovereignty, and draws the eyes of the people somewhat aside from the line royal. But for democracies, they need it not; and they are commonly more quiet and less subject to sedition, than where there are stirps of nobles. For men's eyes are upon the business, and not upon the persons; or if upon the persons, it is for the business' sake, as fittest, and not for flags and pedigree. We see the Switzers last well, notwithstanding their diversity of religion and of cantons. For utility is their bond, and not respects. The united provinces of the Low Countries in their government excel; for where there is an equality, the consultations are more indifferent, and the payments and tributes more cheerful. A great and potent nobility addeth majesty to a monarch, but diminisheth power; and putteth life and spirit into the people, but presseth their fortune. It is well when nobles are not too great for sovereignty, nor for justice; and yet maintained in that height, as the insolency of inferiors may be broken upon them before it come on too fast upon the majesty of kings. A numerous nobility causeth poverty and inconvenience in a state; for it is a surcharge of expense; and besides, it being of necessity that many of the nobility fall in time to be weak in fortune, it maketh a kind of disproportion between honour and means.

As for nobility in particular persons; it is a reverend thing to see an ancient castle or building not in decay, or to see a fair timber-tree sound and perfect: how much more to behold an ancient noble family, which hath stood against the waves and weathers of time. For new

40

Of Nobility

nobility is but the act of power; but ancient nobility is
the act of time. Those that are first raised to nobility
are commonly more virtuous, but less innocent, than
their descendants; for there is rarely any rising but by
a commixture of good and evil arts. But it is reason
the memory of their virtues remain to their posterity,
and their faults die with themselves. Nobility of birth
commonly abateth industry; and he that is not industrious envieth him that is. Besides, noble persons
cannot go much higher; and he that standeth at a stay,
when others rise, can hardly avoid motions of envy.
On the other side, nobility extinguisheth the passive
envy from others towards them; because they are in
possession of honour. Certainly, kings that have able
men of their nobility shall find ease in employing them,
and a better slide in their business; for people
naturally bend to them, as born in some sort to command.

Essay XV.—OF SEDITIONS AND TROUBLES

SHEPHERDS of people had need know the kalendars of tempests in state; which are commonly greatest when things grow to equality; as natural tempests are greatest about the *Æquinoctia*. And as there are certain hollow blasts of wind and secret swellings of seas before a tempest, so are there in states:

—Ille etiam cæcos instare tumultus
Sæpe monet, fraudesque et operta tumescere bella.

Libels and licentious discourses against the state, when they are frequent and open; and in like sort, false news, often running up and down, to the disadvantage of the state, and hastily embraced; are amongst the signs of troubles. Virgil, giving the pedigree of Fame, saith *she was sister to the Giants :*

Illam Terra parens, irâ irritata Deorum,
Extremam (ut perhibent) Cæo Enceladoque sororem
Progenuit.—

As if fames were the relics of seditions past; but they are no less, indeed, the preludes of seditions to come. Howsoever, he noteth it right, that seditious tumults and seditious fames differ no more but as brother and sister, masculine and feminine; especially if it come to that, that the best actions of a state, and the most plausible, and which ought to give greatest contentment, are taken in ill sense, and traduced: for that shews the envy great, as Tacitus saith, *Conflatâ magnâ invidiâ, seu bene seu male gesta premunt.* Neither doth it follow, that because these fames are a sign of troubles, that the suppressing of them with too much severity should be a remedy of troubles. For the despising of them many

times checks them best; and the going about to stop
them doth but make a wonder long-lived. Also that
kind of obedience, which Tacitus speaketh of, is to be
held suspected: *Erant in officio, sed tamen qui mallent
mandata imperantium interpretari, quam exequi:* disputing, excusing, cavilling upon mandates and directions, is a kind of shaking off the yoke, and assay of
disobedience; especially if in those disputings they
which are for the direction speak fearfully and tenderly,
and those that are against it audaciously.

Also, as Machiavel noteth well, when princes, that
ought to be common parents, make themselves as a
party, and lean to a side, it is as a boat that is overthrown by uneven weight on the one side; as was well
seen in the time of Henry the Third of France; for first
himself entered league for the extirpation of the Protestants, and presently after the same league was turned
upon himself. For when the authority of princes is
made but an accessary to a cause, and that there be
other bands that tie faster than the band of sovereignty,
kings begin to be put almost out of possession.

Also, when discords and quarrels and factions are
carried openly and audaciously, it is a sign the reverence
of government is lost. For the motions of the greatest
persons in a government ought to be as the motions of
the planets under *primum mobile,* according to the old
opinion, which is, that every of them is carried swiftly
by the highest motion, and softly in their own motion.
And therefore, when great ones in their own particular
motion move violently, and, as Tacitus expresseth it
well, *liberius quam ut imperantium meminissent,* it is a
sign the orbs are out of frame. For reverence is that
wherewith princes are girt from God, who threateneth
the dissolving thereof: *Solvam cingula regum.*

So when any of the four pillars of government are
mainly shaken or weakened (which are religion,
justice, counsel, and treasure), men had need to pray for
fair weather. But let us pass from this part of predictions (concerning which, nevertheless, more light may
be taken from that which followeth), and let us speak

43

first of the materials of seditions; then of the motives of them; and thirdly of the remedies.

Concerning the materials of seditions. It is a thing well to be considered; for the surest way to prevent seditions (if the times do bear it) is to take away the matter of them. For if there be fuel prepared, it is hard to tell whence the spark shall come that shall set it on fire. The matter of seditions is of two kinds; much poverty and much discontentment. It is certain, so many overthrown estates, so many votes for troubles. Lucan noteth well the state of Rome before the civil war:

Hinc usura vorax, rapidumque in tempore fœnus,
Hinc concussa fides, et multis utile bellum.

This same *multis utile bellum* is an assured and infallible sign of a state disposed to seditions and troubles. And if this poverty and broken estate in the better sort be joined with a want and necessity in the mean people, the danger is imminent and great. For the rebellions of the belly are the worst. As for discontentments, they are in the politic body like to humours in the natural, which are apt to gather a preternatural heat and to inflame. And let no prince measure the danger of them by this, whether they be just or unjust; for that were to imagine people to be too reasonable, who do often spurn at their own good: nor yet by this, whether the griefs whereupon they rise be in fact great or small; for they are the most dangerous discontentments where the fear is greater than the feeling. *Dolendi modus, timendi non item.* Besides, in great oppressions, the same things that provoke patience, do withal mate the courage; but in fears it is not so. Neither let any prince or state be secure concerning discontentments, because they have been often, or have been long, and yet no peril hath ensued: for as it is true that every vapour or fume doth not turn into a storm; so it is nevertheless true that storms, though they blow over divers times, yet may fall at last; and, as the Spanish proverb noteth well, *The cord breaketh at the last by the weakest pull.*

Of Seditions and Troubles

The causes and motives of seditions are: innovation in religion; taxes; alteration of laws and customs; breaking of privileges; general oppression; advancement of unworthy persons; strangers; dearths; disbanded soldiers; factions grown desperate; and whatsoever, in offending people, joineth and knitteth them in a common cause.

For the remedies; there may be some general preservatives, whereof we will speak; as for the just cure, it must answer to the particular disease, and so be left to counsel rather than rule.

The first remedy or prevention is to remove by all means possible that material cause of sedition whereof we spake; which is want and poverty in the estate. To which purpose serveth the opening and well-balancing of trade; the cherishing of manufactures; the banishing of idleness; the repressing of waste and excess by sumptuary laws; the improvement and husbanding of the soil: the regulating of prices of things vendible; the moderating of taxes and tributes; and the like. Generally, it is to be foreseen that the population of a kingdom (especially if it be not mown down by wars) do not exceed the stock of the kingdom which should maintain them. Neither is the population to be reckoned only by number; for a smaller number, that spend more and earn less, do wear out an estate sooner than a greater number, that live lower and gather more. Therefore the multiplying nobility and other degrees of quality, in an over-proportion to the common people, doth speedily bring a state to necessity; and so doth likewise an overgrown clergy, for they bring nothing to the stock; and in like manner, when more are bred scholars than preferments can take off.

It is likewise to be remembered that, forasmuch as the increase of any estate must be upon the foreigner (for whatsoever is somewhere gotten is somewhere lost), there be but three things which one nation selleth unto another: the commodity as nature yieldeth it; the manufacture; and the vecture or carriage. So that if these three wheels go, wealth will flow as in a spring tide. And it cometh many times to pass that *materiam superabit opus;* that the work and carriage is more worth than the material, and enricheth a state more; as is notably seen in the Low-Countrymen, who have the best mines above ground in the world.

Above all things, good policy is to be used, that the treasure and moneys in a state be not gathered into few hands. For otherwise a state may have a great stock, and yet starve. And money is like muck, not good except it be spread. This is done chiefly by suppressing, or at the least keeping a strait hand upon the devouring trades of usury, engrossing, great pasturages, and the like.

For removing discontentments, or at least the danger of them. There is in every state (as we know) two portions of subjects, the noblesse and the commonalty. When one of these is discontent, the danger is not great; for common people are of slow motion, if they be not excited by the greater sort; and the greater sort are of small strength, except the multitude be apt and ready to move of themselves. Then is the danger, when the greater sort do but wait for the troubling of the waters amongst the meaner, that then they may declare themselves. The poets feign, that the rest of the gods would have bound Jupiter; which he hearing of, by the counsel of Pallas sent for Briareus, with his hundred hands, to come in to his aid. An emblem, no doubt, to shew how safe it is for monarchs to make sure of the good will of common people.

To give moderate liberty for griefs and discontentments to evaporate (so it be without too great insolency or bravery) is a safe way. For he that turneth the humours back, and maketh the wound bleed inwards, endangereth malign ulcers and pernicious impostumations.

The part of Epimetheus mought well become Prometheus, in the case of discontentments; for there is not a better provision against them. Epimetheus, when griefs and evils flew abroad, at last shut the lid, and kept hope in the bottom of the vessel. Certainly, the politic

Of Seditions and Troubles

and artificial nourishing and entertaining of hopes, and carrying men from hopes to hopes, is one of the best antidotes against the poison of discontentments. And it is a certain sign of a wise government and proceeding when it can hold men's hearts by hopes, when it cannot by satisfaction; and when it can handle things in such manner, as no evil shall appear so peremptory but that it hath some outlet of hope: which is the less hard to do, because both particular persons and factions are apt enough to flatter themselves, or at least to brave that which they believe not.

Also, the foresight and prevention, that there be no likely or fit head whereunto discontented persons may resort, and under whom they may join, is a known but an excellent point of caution. I understand a fit head to be one that hath greatness and reputation; that hath confidence with the discontented party, and upon whom they turn their eyes; and that is thought discontented in his own particular: which kind of persons are either to be won and reconciled to the state, and that in a fast and true manner; or to be fronted with some other of the same party, that may oppose them, and so divide the reputation. Generally, the dividing and breaking of all factions and combinations that are adverse to the state, and setting them at distance or at least distrust amongst themselves, is not one of the worst remedies. For it is a desperate case, if those that hold with the proceeding of the state be full of discord and faction, and those that are against it be entire and united.

I have noted that some witty and sharp speeches which have fallen from princes have given fire to seditions. Cæsar did himself infinite hurt in that speech, *Sylla nescivit litteras, non potuit dictare;* for it did utterly cut off that hope which men had entertained, that he would at one time or other give over his dictatorship. Galba undid himself by that speech, *Legi a se militem, non emi;* for it put the soldiers out of hope of the donative. Probus likewise, by that speech, *Si vixero, non opus erit amplius Romano imperio militidus:* a speech of great despair for the soldiers. And many the like. Surely

47

princes had need, in tender matters and ticklish times, to beware what they say; especially in these short speeches, which fly abroad like darts, and are thought to be shot out of their secret intentions. For as for large discourses, they are flat things, and not so much noted.

Lastly, let princes, against all events, not be without some great person, one or rather more, of military valour, near unto them, for the repressing of seditions in their beginnings. For without that, there useth to be more trepidation in court upon the first breaking out of troubles than were fit. And the state runneth the danger of that which Tacitus saith: *Atque is habitus animorum fuit, ut pessimum facinus auderent pauci, plures vellent, omnes paterentur.* But let such military persons be assured, and well reputed of, rather than factious and popular; holding also good correspondence with the other great men in the state; or else the remedy is worse than the disease.

think that there were no such thing as God, why should they trouble themselves? Epicurus is charged that he did but dissemble for his credit's sake, when he affirmed there were blessed natures, but such as enjoyed themselves without having respect to the government of the world. Wherein they say he did temporise, though in secret he thought there was no God. But certainly he is traduced; for his words are noble and divine: *Non deos vulgi negare profanum, sed vulgi opiniones diis applicare profanum.* Plato could have said no more. And although he had the confidence to deny the administration, he had not the power to deny the nature. The Indians of the West have names for their particular gods, though they have no name for God: as if the heathens should have had the names Jupiter, Apollo, Mars, &c., but not the word *Deus :* which shews that even those barbarous people have the notion, though they have not the latitude and extent of it. So that against atheists the very savages take part with the very subtilest philosophers. The contemplative atheist is rare; a Diagoras, a Bion, a Lucian perhaps, and some others; and yet they seem to be more than they are; for that all that impugn a received religion, or superstition, are, by the adverse part, branded with the name of atheists. But the great atheists indeed are hypocrites; which are ever handling holy things, but without feeling; so as they must needs be cauterized in the end. The causes of atheism are: divisions in religion, if they be many; for any one main division addeth zeal to both sides, but many divisions introduce atheism. Another is, scandal of priests; when it is come to that which S. Bernard saith: *Non est jam dicere, ut populus, sic sacerdos ; quia nec sic populus, ut sacerdos.* A third is, custom of profane scoffing in holy matters, which doth by little and little deface the reverence of religion. And lastly, learned times, specially with peace and prosperity; for troubles and adversities do more bow men's minds to religion. They that deny a God destroy man's nobility; for certainly man is of kin to the beasts by his body; and if he be not of kin to God by his spirit, he

Of Atheism

is a base and ignoble creature. It destroys likewise magnanimity, and the raising of human nature; for take an example of a dog, and mark what a generosity and courage he will put on when he finds himself maintained by a man, who to him is in stead of a god, or *melior natura;* which courage is manifestly such as that creature, without that confidence of a better nature than his own, could never attain. So man, when he resteth and assureth himself upon divine protection and favour, gathereth a force and faith which human nature in itself could not obtain. Therefore, as atheism is in all respects hateful, so in this, that it depriveth human nature of the means to exalt itself above human frailty. As it is in particular persons, so it is in nations: never was there such a state for magnanimity as Rome: of this state hear what Cicero saith: *Quam volumus licet, patres conscripti, nos amemus, tamen nec numero Hispanos, nec robore Gallos, nec calliditate Pœnos, nec artibus Græcos, nec denique hoc ipso hujus gentis et terræ domestico nativoque sensu Italos ipsos et Latinos; sed pietate, ac religione, atque hâc unâ sapientiâ, quod Deorum immortalium numine omnia regi gubernarique perspeximus, omnes gentes nationesque superavimus.*

Essay XVII.—OF SUPERSTITION

It were better to have no opinion of God at all, than such an opinion as is unworthy of him: for the one is unbelief, the other is contumely: and certainly superstition is the reproach of the Deity. Plutarch saith well to that purpose: *Surely* (saith he) *I had rather a great deal men should say there was no such man at all as Plutarch, than that they should say that there was one Plutarch that would eat his children as soon as they were born;* as the poets speak of Saturn. And as the contumely is greater towards God, so the danger is greater towards men. Atheism leaves a man to sense, to philosophy, to natural piety, to laws, to reputation; all which may be guides to an outward moral virtue, though religion were not; but superstition dismounts all these, and erecteth an absolute monarchy in the minds of men. Therefore atheism did never perturb states; for it makes men wary of themselves, as looking no further: and we see the times inclined to atheism (as the time of Augustus Cæsar) were civil times. But superstition hath been the confusion of many states, and bringeth in a new *primum mobile,* that ravisheth all the spheres of government. The master of superstition is the people; and in all superstition wise men follow fools; and arguments are fitted to practice, in a reversed order. It was gravely said by some of the prelates in the Council of Trent, where the doctrine of the schoolmen bare great sway, *that the schoolmen were like astronomers, which did feign eccentrics and epicycles, and such engines of orbs, to save the phenomena, though they knew there were no such things;* and in like manner, that the schoolmen had framed a number of subtile and intricate axioms and theorems, to save the practice of the church. The causes of superstition are: pleasing and sensual rites and ceremonies;

Of Superstition

excess of outward and pharisaical holiness; over-great reverence of traditions, which cannot but load the church; the stratagems of prelates for their own ambition and lucre; the favouring too much of good intentions, which openeth the gate to conceits and novelties; the taking an aim at divine matters by human, which cannot but breed mixture of imaginations; and lastly, barbarous times, especially joined with calamities and disasters. Superstition, without a veil, is a deformed thing; for, as it addeth deformity to an ape to be so like a man, so the similitude of superstition to religion makes it the more deformed. And as wholesome meat corrupteth to little worms, so good forms and orders corrupt into a number of petty observances. There is a superstition in avoiding superstition, when men think to do best if they go furthest from the superstition formerly received: therefore care would be had that (as it fareth in ill purgings) the good be not taken away with the bad; which commonly is done, when the people is the reformer.

Essay XVIII.—OF TRAVEL

TRAVEL, in the younger sort, is a part of education; in the elder, a part of experience. He that travelleth into a country before he hath some entrance into the language, goeth to school, and not to travel. That young men travel under some tutor, or grave servant, I allow well; so that he be such a one that hath the language and hath been in the country before; whereby he may be able to tell them what things are worthy to be seen in the country where they go; what acquaintances they are to seek; what exercises or discipline the place yieldeth. For else young men shall go hooded, and look abroad little. It is a strange thing that in sea-voyages, where there is nothing to be seen but sky and sea, men should make diaries, but in land-travel, wherein so much is to be observed, for the most part they omit it; as if chance were fitter to be registered than observation. Let diaries, therefore, be brought in use. The things to be seen and observed are: the courts of princes, specially when they give audience to ambassadors; the courts of justice, while they sit and hear causes, and so of consistories ecclesiastic; the churches and monasteries, with the monuments which are therein extant; the walls and fortifications of cities and towns, and so the havens and harbours; antiquities and ruins; libraries; colleges, disputations, and lectures, where any are; shipping and navies; houses and gardens of state and pleasure, near great cities; armories; arsenals; magazines; exchanges; burses; warehouses; exercises of horsemanship, fencing, training of soldiers, and the like; comedies, such whereunto the better sort of persons do resort; treasuries of jewels and robes; cabinets and rarities; and, to conclude, whatsoever is memorable in the places where they go. After all which the tutors or servants ought to make

Of Travel

diligent enquiry. As for triumphs, masques, feasts, weddings, funerals, capital executions, and such shews, men need not to be put in mind of them; yet are they not to be neglected. If you will have a young man to put his travel into a little room, and in short time to gather much, this you must do. First, as was said, he must have some entrance into the language, before he goeth. Then he must have such a servant, or tutor, as knoweth the country, as was likewise said. Let him carry with him also some card or book describing the country where he travelleth; which will be a good key to his enquiry. Let him keep also a diary. Let him not stay long in one city or town; more or less as the place deserveth, but not long: nay, when he stayeth in one city or town, let him change his lodging from one end and part of the town to another; which is a great adamant of acquaintance. Let him sequester himself from the company of his countrymen, and diet in such places where there is good company of the nation where he travelleth. Let him, upon his removes from one place to another, procure recommendation to some person of quality residing in the place whither he removeth; that he may use his favour in those things he desireth to see or know. Thus he may abridge his travel with much profit. As for the acquaintance which is to be sought in travel; that which is most of all profitable is acquaintance with the secretaries and employed men of ambassadors; for so in travelling in one country he shall suck the experience of many. Let him also see and visit eminent persons in all kinds, which are of great name abroad; that he may be able to tell how the life agreeth with the fame. For quarrels, they are with care and discretion to be avoided: they are commonly for mistresses, healths, place, and words. And let a man beware how he keepeth company with choleric and quarrelsome persons; for they will engage him into their own quarrels. When a traveller returneth home, let him not leave the countries where he hath travelled altogether behind him, but maintain a correspondence by letters with those of his acquaintance

answer of Apollonius to Vespasian is full of excellent instruction. Vespasian asked him, *What was Nero's overthrow?* He answered: *Nero could touch and tune the harp well; but in government, sometimes he used to wind the pins too high, sometimes to let them down too low.* And certain it is that nothing destroyeth authority so much as the unequal and untimely interchange of power pressed too far, and relaxed too much.

This is true, that the wisdom of all these latter times in princes' affairs is rather fine deliveries and shiftings of dangers and mischiefs when they are near, than solid and grounded courses to keep them aloof. But this is but to try masteries with fortune: and let men beware how they neglect and suffer matter of trouble to be prepared: for no man can forbid the spark, nor tell whence it may come. The difficulties in princes' business are many and great; but the greatest difficulty is often in their own mind. For it is common with princes (saith Tacitus) to will contradictories: *Sunt plerumque regum voluntates vehementes, et inter se contrariæ* For it is the solecism of power, to think to command the end, and yet not to endure the mean.

Kings have to deal with their neighbours, their wives, their children, their prelates or clergy, their nobles, their second-nobles or gentlemen, their merchants, their commons, and their men of war; and from all these arise dangers, if care and circumspection be not used.

First for their neighbours; there can no general rule be given (the occasions are so variable), save one, which ever holdeth; which is, that princes do keep due sentinel, that none of their neighbours do overgrow so (by increase of territory, by embracing of trade, by approaches, or the like) as they become more able to annoy them than they were. And this is generally the work of standing councils to foresee and to hinder it. During that triumvirate of kings, King Henry VIII. of England, Francis the I. King of France, and Charles the V. Emperor, there was such a watch kept, that none of the three could win a palm of ground, but the other two would straightways balance it, either by confederation, or, if need were, by a war; and would not in any wise take up peace at interest. And the like was done by that league (which Guicciardine saith was the security of Italy) made between Ferdinando King of Naples, Lorenzius Medices, and Ludovicus Sforza, potentates, the one of Florence, the other of Milan. Neither is the opinion of some of the schoolmen to be received, *that a war cannot justly be made but upon a precedent injury or provocation.* For there is no question but a just fear of an imminent danger, though there be no blow given, is a lawful cause of a war.

For their wives; there are cruel examples of them. Livia is infamed for the poisoning of her husband; Roxolana, Solyman's wife, was the destruction of that renowned prince, Sultan Mustapha, and otherwise troubled his house and succession; Edward the Second of England his queen had the principal hand in the deposing and murther of her husband. This kind of danger is then to be feared, chiefly, when the wives have plots for the raising of their own children, or else that they be advoutresses.

For their children; the tragedies, likewise, of dangers from them have been many. And generally, the entering of fathers into suspicion of their children hath been ever unfortunate. The destruction of Mustapha (that we named before) was so fatal to Solyman's line, as the succession of the Turks, from Solyman until this day, is suspected to be untrue and of strange blood; for that Selymus the Second was thought to be supposititious. The destruction of Crispus, a young prince of rare towardness, by Constantinus the Great, his father, was in like manner fatal to his house; for both Constantinus and Constance, his sons, died violent deaths; and Constantius, his other son, did little better; who died, indeed, of sickness, but after that Julianus had taken arms against him. The destruction of Demetrius, son to Philip the Second of Macedon, turned upon the father, who died of repentance. And many like examples there are; but few or none where the fathers had good by such distrust; except it were where the sons were up in open arms against them; as was Selymus the First against Bajazet; and the three sons of Henry the Second, King of England.

For their prelates; when they are proud and great, there is also danger from them: as it was in the times of Anselmus and Thomas Becket, Archbishops of Canterbury; who with their crosiers did almost try it with the king's sword; and yet they had to deal with stout and haughty kings, William Rufus, Henry the First, and Henry the Second. The danger is not from that state, but where it hath a dependence of foreign authority; or where the churchmen come in and are elected, not by the collation of the king, or particular patrons, but by the people.

For their nobles; to keep them at a distance, it is not amiss; but to depress them may make a king more absolute, but less safe, and less able to perform anything that he desires. I have noted it in my history of King Henry the Seventh of England, who depressed his nobility; whereupon it came to pass that his times were full of difficulties and troubles; for the nobility, though they continued loyal unto him, yet did they not co-operate with him in his business. So that, in effect, he was fain to do all things himself.

For their second-nobles; there is not much danger from them, being a body dispersed. They may sometimes discourse high, but that doth little hurt; besides, they are a counterpoise to the higher nobility, that they grow not too potent; and lastly, being the most immediate in authority with the common people, they do best temper popular commotions.

For their merchants; they are *vena porta ;* and if they flourish not, a kingdom may have good limbs, but will have empty veins, and nourish little. Taxes and imposts upon them do seldom good to the king's revenue; for that that he wins in the hundred he leeseth in the shire; the particular rates being increased, but the total bulk of trading rather decreased.

For their commons; there is little danger from them, except it be where they have great and potent heads;

Of Empire

or where you meddle with the point of religion, or their customs, or means of life.

For their men of war; it is a dangerous state where they live and remain in a body, and are used to donatives; whereof we see examples in the janizaries, and pretorian bands of Rome: but trainings of men, and arming them in several places, and under several commanders, and without donatives, are things of defence, and no danger.

Princes are like to heavenly bodies, which cause good or evil times; and which have much veneration, but no rest. All precepts concerning kings are in effect comprehended in those two remembrances: *Memento quod es homo*, and *Memento quod es Deus*, or *vice Dei :* the one bridleth their power, and the other their will.

Essay XX.—OF COUNSEL

THE greatest trust between man and man is the trust of giving counsel. For in other confidences men commit the parts of life; their lands, their goods, their children, their credit, some particular affair; but to such as they make their counsellors, they commit the whole: by how much the more they are obliged to all faith and integrity. The wisest princes need not think it any diminution to their greatness, or derogation to their sufficiency, to rely upon counsel. God himself is not without, but hath made it one of the great names of his blessed Son; *The Counsellor*. Salomon hath pronounced that *in counsel is stability*. Things will have their first or second agitation; if they be not tossed upon the arguments of counsel, they will be tossed upon the waves of fortune, and be full of inconstancy, doing and undoing, like the reeling of a drunken man. Salomon's son found the force of counsel, as his father saw the necessity of it. For the beloved kingdom of God was first rent and broken by ill counsel; upon which counsel there are set, for our instruction, the two marks whereby bad counsel is for ever best discerned: that it was young counsel, for the persons; and violent counsel, for the matter.

The ancient times do set forth in figure both the incorporation and inseparable conjunction of counsel with kings, and the wise and politic use of counsel by kings: the one, in that they say Jupiter did marry Metis, which signifieth counsel; whereby they intend that sovereignty is married to counsel: the other in that which followeth, which was thus: they say, after Jupiter was married to Metis, she conceived by him and was with child; but Jupiter suffered her not to stay till she brought forth, but eat her up; whereby he became himself with child, and was delivered of Pallas

Of Counsel

armed, out of his head. Which monstrous fable containeth a secret of empire; how kings are to make use of their counsel of state. That first they ought to refer matters unto them, which is the first begetting or impregnation; but when they are elaborate, moulded, and shaped in the womb of their counsel, and grow ripe and ready to be brought forth, that then they suffer not their counsel to go through with the resolution and direction, as if it depended on them; but take the matter back into their own hands, and make it appear to the world that the decrees and final directions (which, because they come forth with prudence and power, are resembled to Pallas armed) proceeded from themselves; and not only from their authority, but (the more to add reputation to themselves) from their head and device.

Let us now speak of the inconveniences of counsel, and of the remedies. The inconveniences that have been noted in calling and using counsel are three. First, the revealing of affairs, whereby they become less secret. Secondly, the weakening of the authority of princes, as if they were less of themselves. Thirdly, the danger of being unfaithfully counselled, and more for the good of them that counsel than of him that is counselled. For which inconveniences, the doctrine of Italy, and practice of France, in some kings' times, hath introduced cabinet counsels; a remedy worse than the disease.

As to secrecy; princes are not bound to communicate all matters with all counsellors, but may extract and select. Neither is it necessary that he that consulteth what he should do, should declare what he will do. But let princes beware that the unsecreting of their affairs comes not from themselves. And as for cabinet counsels, it may be their motto, *Plenus rimarum sum :* one futile person, that maketh it his glory to tell, will do more hurt than many, that know it their duty to conceal. It is true there be some affairs which require extreme secrecy, which will hardly go beyond one or two persons besides the king: neither are those counsels unprosperous; for, besides the secrecy, they commonly go on constantly in one spirit of direction, without distraction. But then it must be a prudent king, such as is able to grind with a hand-mill; and those inward counsellors had need also be wise men, and especially true and trusty to the king's ends; as it was with King Henry the Seventh of England, who in his greatest business imparted himself to none, except it were to Morton and Fox.

For weakening of authority; the fable sheweth the remedy. Nay, the majesty of kings is rather exalted than diminished when they are in the chair of counsel: neither was there ever prince bereaved of his dependences by his counsel, except where there hath been either an over-greatness in one counsellor or an over-strict combination in divers; which are things soon found and holpen.

For the last inconvenience, that men will counsel with an eye to themselves; certainly, *non inveniet fidem super terram* is meant of the nature of times, and not of all particular persons. There be that are in nature faithful, and sincere, and plain, and direct, not crafty and involved; let princes, above all, draw to themselves such natures. Besides, counsellors are not commonly so united, but that one counsellor keepeth sentinel over another; so that if any do counsel out of faction or private ends, it commonly comes to the king's ear. But the best remedy is, if princes know their counsellors as well as their counsellors know them:

Principis est virtus maxima nosse suos.

And on the other side, counsellors should not be too speculative into their sovereign's person. The true composition of a counsellor is rather to be skilful in their master's business than in his nature; for then he is like to advise him, and not to feed his humour. It is of singular use to princes if they take the opinions of their counsel both separately and together. For private opinion is more free, but opinion before others is more reverend. In private, men are more bold in their own humours; and in consort, men are more obnoxious to others' humours. Therefore it is good to take both: and of the inferior sort rather in private, to preserve freedom; of the greater rather in consort, to preserve respect. It is in vain for princes to take counsel concerning matters, if they take no counsel likewise concerning persons; for all matters are as dead images, and the life of the execution of affairs resteth in the good choice of persons. Neither is it enough to consult concerning persons *secundum genera,* as in an idea or mathematical description, what the kind and character of the person should be; for the greatest errors are committed, and the most judgement is shewn, in the choice of individuals. It was truly said, *Optimi consiliarii mortui :* books will speak plain when counsellors blanch. Therefore it is good to be conversant in them, specially the books of such as themselves have been actors upon the stage.

The counsels at this day in most places are but familiar meetings, where matters are rather talked on than debated. And they run too swift to the order or act of counsel. It were better that, in causes of weight, the matter were propounded one day and not spoken to till the next day; *in nocte consilium.* So was it done in the commission of union between England and Scotland, which was a grave and orderly assembly. I commend set days for petitions; for both it gives the suitors more certainty for their attendance, and it frees the meetings for matters of estate, that they may *hoc agere.* In choice of committees for ripening business for the counsel, it is better to choose indifferent persons, than to make an indifferency by putting in those that are strong on both sides. I commend also standing commissions; as for trade, for treasure, for war, for suits, for some provinces; for where there be divers particular counsels, and but one counsel of estate (as it is in Spain), they are, in effect, no more than standing commissions, save that they have greater authority. Let such as are to inform counsels out of their particular professions (as lawyers, seamen, mintmen, and the like) be first heard before

Essay XXI.—OF DELAY

FORTUNE is like the market; where many times, if you can stay a little, the price will fall. And again, it is sometimes like Sibylla's offer; which at first offereth the commodity at full, then consumeth part and part, and still holdeth up the price. For *Occasion* (as it is in the common verse) *turneth a bald noddle, after she hath presented her locks in front, and no hold taken;* or at least turneth the handle of the bottle first to be received, and after the belly, which is hard to clasp. There is surely no greater wisdom than well to time the beginnings and onsets of things. Dangers are no more light, if they once seem light; and more dangers have deceived men than forced them. Nay, it were better to meet some dangers half way, though they come nothing near, than to keep too long a watch upon their approaches; for if a man watch too long, it is odds he will fall asleep. On the other side, to be deceived with too long shadows (as some have been when the moon was low and shone on their enemy's back), and so to shoot off before the time; or to teach dangers to come on, by over-early buckling towards them; is another extreme. The ripeness or unripeness of the occasion (as we said) must ever be well weighed; and generally it is good to commit the beginnings of all great actions to Argus with his hundred eyes, and the ends to Briareus with his hundred hands: first to watch, and then to speed. For the helmet of Pluto, which maketh the politic man go invisible, is secrecy in the counsel and celerity in the execution. For when things are once come to the execution, there is no secrecy comparable to celerity; like the motion of a bullet in the air, which flieth so swift as it outruns the eye.

Essay XXII.—OF CUNNING

WE take cunning for a sinister or crooked wisdom. And certainly there is a great difference between a cunning man and a wise man; not only in point of honesty, but in point of ability. There be that can pack the cards, and yet cannot play well; so there are some that are good in canvasses and factions, that are otherwise weak men. Again, it is one thing to understand persons, and another thing to understand matters; for many are perfect in men's humours, that are not greatly capable of the real part of business; which is the constitution of one that hath studied men more than books. Such men are fitter for practice than for counsel; and they are good but in their own alley: turn them to new men, and they have lost their aim; so as the old rule to know a fool from a wise man, *Mitte ambos nudos ad ignotos et videbis,* doth scarce hold for them. And because these cunning men are like haberdashers of small wares, it is not amiss to set forth their shop.

It is a point of cunning, to wait upon him with whom you speak, with your eye, as the Jesuits give it in precept; for there be many wise men that have secret hearts and transparent countenances. Yet this would be done with a demure abasing of your eye sometimes, as the Jesuits also do use.

Another is, that when you have anything to obtain of present dispatch, you entertain and amuse the party with whom you deal with some other discourse, that he be not too much awake to make objections. I knew a counsellor and secretary, that never came to Queen Elizabeth of England with bills to sign, but he would always first put her into some discourse of estate, that she mought the less mind the bills.

The like surprise may be made by moving things when the party is in haste, and cannot stay to consider advisedly of that is moved.

Of Cunning

If a man would cross a business that he doubts some other would handsomely and effectually move, let him pretend to wish it well, and move it himself in such sort as may foil it.

The breaking off in the midst of that one was about to say, as if he took himself up, breeds a greater appetite in him with whom you confer to know more.

And because it works better when anything seemeth to be gotten from you by question, than if you offer it of yourself, you may lay a bait for a question, by shewing another visage and countenance than you are wont; to the end to give occasion for the party to ask what the matter is of the change? As Nehemias did: *And I had not before that time been sad before the king.*

In things that are tender and unpleasing, it is good to break the ice by some whose words are of less weight, and to reserve the more weighty voice to come in as by chance, so that he may be asked the question upon the other's speech. As Narcissus did, in relating to Claudius the marriage of Messalina and Silius.

In things that a man would not be seen in himself, it is a point of cunning to borrow the name of the world; as to say, *The world says,* or, *There is a speech abroad.*

I knew one that, when he wrote a letter, he would put that which was most material in the postscript, as if it had been a by-matter.

I knew another that, when he came to have speech, he would pass over that that he intended most, and go forth, and come back again, and speak of it as of a thing that he had almost forgot.

Some procure themselves to be surprised at such times as it is like the party that they work upon will suddenly come upon them, and to be found with a letter in their hand, or doing somewhat which they are not accustomed; to the end they may be apposed of those things which of themselves they are desirous to utter.

It is a point of cunning, to let fall those words in a man's own name, which he would have another man learn and use, and thereupon take advantage. I knew two that were competitors for the secretary's place in

Queen Elizabeth's time, and yet kept good quarter between themselves, and would confer one with another upon the business; and the one of them said, That to be a secretary in the *declination of a monarchy* was a ticklish thing, and that he did not affect it: the other straight caught up those words, and discoursed with divers of his friends, that he had no reason to desire to be secretary in the *declination of a monarchy*. The first man took hold of it, and found means it was told the Queen; who, hearing of a *declination of a monarchy*, took it so ill, as she would never after hear of the other's suit.

There is a cunning, which we in England call *The turning of the cat in the pan ;* which is, when that which a man says to another, he lays it as if another had said it to him. And to say truth, it is not easy, when such a matter passed between two, to make it appear from which of them it first moved and began.

It is a way that some men have, to glance and dart at others by justifying themselves by negatives; as to say, *This I do not :* as Tigellinus did towards Burrhus; *Se non diversas spes, sed incolumitatem imperatoris simpliciter spectare.*

Some have in readiness so many tales and stories, as there is nothing they would insinuate, but they can wrap it into a tale; which serveth both to keep themselves more in guard, and to make others carry it with more pleasure.

It is a good point of cunning, for a man to shape the answer he would have in his own words and propositions; for it makes the other party stick the less.

It is strange how long some men will lie in wait to speak somewhat they desire to say and how far about they will fetch, and how many other matters they will beat over, to come near it. It is a thing of great patience, but yet of much use.

A sudden, bold, and unexpected question doth many times surprise a man, and lay him open. Like to him, that having changed his name, and walking in Paul's, another suddenly came behind him and called him

Of Cunning

by his true name, whereat straightways he looked back.

But these small wares and petty points of cunning are infinite; and it were a good deed to make a list of them; for that nothing doth more hurt in a state than that cunning men pass for wise.

But certainly some there are that know the resorts and falls of business, that cannot sink into the main of it; like a house that hath convenient stairs and entries, but never a fair room. Therefore you shall see them find out pretty looses in the conclusion, but are no ways able to examine or debate matters. And yet commonly they take advantage of their inability, and would be thought wits of direction. Some build rather upon the abusing of others, and (as we now say) *putting tricks upon them,* than upon soundness of their own proceedings. But Salomon saith: *Prudens advertit ad gressus suos : stultus divertit ad dolos.*

Essay XXIII.—OF WISDOM FOR A MAN'S SELF

An ant is a wise creature for itself, but it is a shrewd thing in an orchard or garden. And certainly men that are great lovers of themselves waste the public. Divide with reason between self-love and society; and be so true to thyself, as thou be not false to others, specially to thy king and country. It is a poor centre of a man's actions, himself. It is right earth. For that only stands fast upon his own centre; whereas all things that have affinity with the heavens move upon the centre of another, which they benefit. The referring of all to a man's self is more tolerable in a sovereign prince; because themselves are not only themselves, but their good and evil is at the peril of the public fortune. But it is a desperate evil in a servant to a prince, or a citizen in a republic. For whatsoever affairs pass such a man's hands, he crooketh them to his own ends; which must needs be often eccentric to the ends of his master or state. Therefore let princes, or states, choose such servants as have not this mark; except they mean their service should be made but the accessary. That which maketh the effect more pernicious is that all proportion is lost. It were disproportion enough for the servant's good to be preferred before the master's; but yet it is a greater extreme, when a little good of the servant shall carry things against a great good of the master's. And yet that is the case of bad officers, treasurers, ambassadors, generals, and other false and corrupt servants; which set a bias upon their bowl, of their own petty ends and envies, to the overthrow of their master's great and important affairs. And for the most part, the good such servants receive is after the model of their own fortune; but the hurt they sell for that good is after the

Of Wisdom for a Man's Self

model of their master's fortune. And certainly it is the nature of extreme self-lovers, as they will set an house on fire, and it were but to roast their eggs; and yet these men many times hold credit with their masters, because their study is but to please them and profit themselves; and for either respect they will abandon the good of their affairs.

Wisdom for a man's self is, in many branches thereof, a depraved thing. It is the wisdom of rats, that will be sure to leave a house somewhat before it fall. It is the wisdom of the fox, that thrusts out the badger, who digged and made room for him. It is the wisdom of crocodiles, that shed tears when they would devour. But that which is specially to be noted is, that those which (as Cicero says of Pompey) are *sui amantes sine rivali*, are many times unfortunate. And whereas they have all their time sacrificed to themselves, they become in the end themselves sacrifices to the inconstancy of fortune, whose wings they thought by their self-wisdom to have pinioned.

Essay XXIV.—OF INNOVATIONS

As the births of living creatures at first are ill-shapen, so are all innovations, which are the births of time. Yet notwithstanding, as those that first bring honour into their family are commonly more worthy than most that succeed, so the first precedent (if it be good) is seldom attained by imitation. For ill, to man's nature as it stands perverted, hath a natural motion, strongest in continuance; but good, as a forced motion, strongest at first. Surely every medicine is an innovation; and he that will not apply new remedies must expect new evils: for time is the greatest innovator; and if time of course alter things to the worse, and wisdom and counsel shall not alter them to the better, what shall be the end? It is true, that what is settled by custom, though it be not good, yet at least it is fit. And those things which have long gone together are as it were confederate within themselves: whereas new things piece not so well; but though they help by their utility, yet they trouble by their inconformity. Besides, they are like strangers, more admired and less favoured. All this is true, if time stood still; which contrariwise moveth so round, that a froward retention of custom is as turbulent a thing as an innovation; and they that reverence too much old times are but a scorn to the new. It were good therefore that men in their innovations would follow the example of time itself, which indeed innovateth greatly, but quietly and by degrees scarce to be perceived: for otherwise, whatsoever is new is unlooked for; and ever it mends some, and pairs other: and he that is holpen takes it for a fortune, and thanks the time; and he that is hurt, for a wrong, and imputeth it to the author. It is good also not to try experiments in states, except the necessity be urgent, or the utility evident; and well to beware that it be the

Of Innovations

reformation that draweth on the change, and not the desire of change that pretendeth the reformation. And lastly, that the novelty, though it be not rejected, yet be held for a suspect; and, as the Scripture saith, *that we make a stand upon the ancient way, and then look about us, and discover what is the straight and right way, and so to walk in it.*

Essay XXV.—OF DISPATCH

AFFECTED dispatch is one of the most dangerous things to business that can be. It is like that which the physicians call pre-digestion, or hasty digestion, which is sure to fill the body full of crudities and secret seeds of diseases. Therefore measure not dispatch by the times of sitting, but by the advancement of the business. And as in races it is not the large stride or high lift that makes the speed; so in business, the keeping close to the matter, and not taking of it too much at once, procureth dispatch. It is the care of some only to come off speedily for the time, or to contrive some false periods of business, because they may seem men of dispatch. But it is one thing to abbreviate by contracting, another by cutting off: and business so handled at several sittings or meetings goeth commonly backward and forward in an unsteady manner. I knew a wise man that had it for a by-word, when he saw men hasten to a conclusion: *Stay a little, that we may make an end the sooner*.

On the other side, true dispatch is a rich thing. For time is the measure of business, as money is of wares; and business is bought at a dear hand where there is small dispatch. The Spartans and Spaniards have been noted to be of small dispatch: *Mi venga la muerte de Spagna; Let my death come from Spain;* for then it will be sure to be long in coming.

Give good hearing to those that give the first information in business; and rather direct them in the beginning than interrupt them in the continuance of their speeches: for he that is put out of his own order will go forward and backward, and be more tedious while he waits upon his memory than he could have been if he had gone on in his own course. But sometimes it is seen that the moderator is more troublesome than the actor.

76

Of Dispatch

Iterations are commonly loss of time: but there is no such gain of time as to iterate often the state of the question; for it chaseth away many a frivolous speech as it is coming forth. Long and curious speeches are as fit for dispatch, as a robe or mantle with a long train is for race. Prefaces, and passages, and excusations, and other speeches of reference to the person, are great wastes of time; and though they seem to proceed of modesty, they are bravery. Yet beware of being too material, when there is any impediment or obstruction in men's wills; for preoccupation of mind ever requireth preface of speech; like a fomentation to make the unguent enter.

Above all things, order, and distribution, and singling out of parts, is the life of dispatch; so as the distribution be not too subtile: for he that doth not divide will never enter well into business; and he that divideth too much will never come out of it clearly. To choose time is to save time; and an unseasonable motion is but beating the air. There be three parts of business: the preparation, the debate or examination, and the perfection. Whereof, if you look for dispatch, let the middle only be the work of many, and the first and last the work of few. The proceeding upon somewhat conceived in writing doth for the most part facilitate dispatch: for though it should be wholly rejected, yet that negative is more pregnant of direction than an indefinite; as ashes are more generative than dust.

Essay XXVI.—OF SEEMING WISE

It hath been an opinion that the French are wiser than they seem, and the Spaniards seem wiser than they are. But howsoever it be between nations, certainly it is so between man and man. For as the Apostle saith of godliness, *Having a shew of godliness, but denying the power thereof;* so certainly there are in point of wisdom and sufficiency that do nothing or little very solemnly: *magno conatu nugas.* It is a ridiculous thing and fit for a satire to persons of judgement, to see what shifts these formalists have, and what prospectives to make superficies to seem body that hath depth and bulk. Some are so close and reserved as they will not shew their wares but by a dark light, and seem always to keep back somewhat; and when they know within themselves they speak of that they do not well know, would nevertheless seem to others to know of that which they may not well speak. Some help themselves with countenance and gesture, and are wise by signs; as Cicero saith of Piso, that when he answered him he fetched one of his brows up to his forehead, and bent the other down to his chin: *Respondes, altero ad frontem sublato, altero ad mentum depresso supercilio, crudelitatem tibi non placere.* Some think to bear it by speaking a great word and being peremptory; and go on, and take by admittance that which they cannot make good. Some, whatsoever is beyond their reach, will seem to despise or make light of it as impertinent or curious; and so would have their ignorance seem judgement. Some are never without a difference, and commonly by amusing men with a subtilty blanch the matter; of whom A. Gellius saith, *hominem delirum, qui verborum minutiis rerum frangit pondera.* Of which kind also Plato, in his *Protagoras,* bringeth in Prodicus in scorn, and maketh him make a speech that consisteth of distinctions from the beginning

Of Seeming Wise

to the end. Generally, such men in all deliberations find ease to be of the negative side, and affect a credit to object and foretell difficulties: for when propositions are denied, there is an end of them; but if they be allowed, it requireth a new work: which false point of wisdom is the bane of business. To conclude, there is no decaying merchant, or inward beggar, hath so many tricks to uphold the credit of their wealth, as these empty persons have to maintain the credit of their sufficiency. Seeming wise men may make shift to get opinion: but let no man choose them for employment; for certainly you were better take for business a man somewhat absurd than over-formal.

Essay XXVII.—OF FRIENDSHIP

It had been hard for him that spake it to have put more truth and untruth together in a few words, than in that speech, *Whosoever is delighted in solitude is either a wild beast or a god.* For it is most true that a natural and secret hatred and aversation towards society, in any man, hath somewhat of the savage beast; but it is most untrue that it should have any character at all of the divine nature; except it proceed, not out of a pleasure in solitude, but out of a love and desire to sequester a man's self for a higher conversation: such as is found to have been falsely and feignedly in some of the heathen; as Epimenides the Candian, Numa the Roman, Empedocles the Sicilian, and Apollonius of Tyana; and truly and really in divers of the ancient hermits and holy fathers of the church. But little do men perceive what solitude is, and how far it extendeth. For a crowd is not company, and faces are but a gallery of pictures, and talk but a tinkling cymbal, where there is no love. The Latin adage meeteth with it a little, *Magna civitas, magna solitudo ;* because in a great town friends are scattered; so that there is not that fellowship, for the most part, which is in less neighbour-hoods. But we may go further and affirm most truly, that it is a mere and miserable solitude to want true friends, without which the world is but a wilderness; and even in this sense also of solitude, whosoever in the frame of his nature and affections is unfit for friendship, he taketh it of the beast, and not from humanity.

A principal fruit of friendship is the ease and dis-charge of the fulness and swellings of the heart, which passions of all kinds do cause and induce. We know diseases of stoppings and suffocations are the most dangerous in the body; and it is not much otherwise in the mind: you may take sarza to open the liver, steel

Of Friendship

to open the spleen, flowers of sulphur for the lungs, castoreum for the brain; but no receipt openeth the heart, but a true friend, to whom you may impart griefs, joys, fears, hopes, suspicions, counsels, and whatsoever lieth upon the heart to oppress it, in a kind of civil shrift or confession.

It is a strange thing to observe how high a rate great kings and monarchs do set upon this fruit of friendship whereof we speak: so great, as they purchase it many times at the hazard of their own safety and greatness. For princes, in regard of the distance of their fortune from that of their subjects and servants, cannot gather this fruit, except (to make themselves capable thereof) they raise some persons to be as it were companions and almost equals to themselves, which many times sorteth to inconvenience. The modern languages give unto such persons the name of *favourites*, or *privadoes*; as if it were matter of grace, or conversation. But the Roman name attaineth the true use and cause thereof, naming them *participes curarum*; for it is that which tieth the knot. And we see plainly that this hath been done, not by weak and passionate princes only, but by the wisest and most politic that ever reigned; who have oftentimes joined to themselves some of their servants, whom both themselves have called *friends*, and allowed others likewise to call them in the same manner, using the word which is received between private men.

L. Sylla, when he commanded Rome, raised Pompey (after surnamed the Great) to that height, that Pompey vaunted himself for Sylla's overmatch. For when he had carried the consulship for a friend of his, against the pursuit of Sylla, and that Sylla did a little resent thereat, and began to speak great, Pompey turned upon him again, and in effect bade him be quiet; *for that more men adored the sun rising than the sun setting*. With Julius Cæsar, Decimus Brutus had obtained that interest, as he set him down in his testament for heir in remainder after his nephew. And this was the man that had power with him to draw him forth to his death. For when Cæsar would have discharged the senate, in regard of some ill presages, and specially a dream of Calpurnia, this man lifted him gently by the arm out of his chair, telling him he hoped he would not dismiss the senate till his wife had dreamt a better dream. And it seemeth his favour was so great, as Antonius, in a letter which is recited *verbatim* in one of Cicero's *Philippics*, calleth him *venefica*, "witch"; as if he had enchanted Cæsar. Augustus raised Agrippa (though of mean birth) to that height, as, when he consulted with Mæcenas about the marriage of his daughter Julia, Mæcenas took the liberty to tell him, *that he must either marry his daughter to Agrippa, or take away his life; there was no third way, he had made him so great.* With Tiberius Cæsar, Sejanus had ascended to that height, as they two were termed and reckoned as a pair of friends. Tiberius in a letter to him saith, *Hæc pro amicitiâ nostrâ non occultavi;* and the whole senate dedicated an altar to Friendship, as to a goddess, in respect of the great dearness of friendship between them two. The like or more was between Septimius Severus and Plautianus. For he forced his eldest son to marry the daughter of Plautianus; and would often maintain Plautianus in doing affronts to his son; and did write also in a letter to the senate by these words: *I love the man so well, as I wish he may over-live me.* Now if these princes had been as a Trajan, or a Marcus Aurelius, a man might have thought that this had proceeded of an abundant goodness of nature; but being men so wise, for such strength and severity of mind, and so extreme lovers of themselves, as all these were, it proveth most plainly that they found their own felicity (though as great as ever happened to mortal men) but as an half piece, except they mought have a friend to make it entire: and yet, which is more, they were princes that had wives, sons, nephews; and yet all these could not supply the comfort of friendship.

It is not to be forgotten, what Commineus observeth of his first master, Duke Charles the Hardy; namely, that he would communicate his secrets with none; and least of all, those secrets which troubled him most. Whereupon he goeth on and saith, that towards his latter

Of Friendship

time *that closeness did impair and a little perish his under-standing*. Surely Commineus mought have made the same judgement also, if it had pleased him, of his second master, Lewis the Eleventh, whose closeness was indeed his tormentor. The parable of Pythagoras is dark, but true; *Cor ne edito*, " Eat not the heart." Certainly, if a man would give it a hard phrase, those that want friends to open themselves unto are cannibals of their own hearts. But one thing is most admirable (wherewith I will conclude this first fruit of friendship), which is, that this communicating of a man's self to his friend works two contrary effects; for it redoubleth joys, and cutteth griefs in halfs. For there is no man that imparteth his joys to his friend, but he joyeth the more; and no man that imparteth his griefs to his friend, but he grieveth the less. So that it is in truth of operation upon a man's mind, of like virtue as the alchymists use to attribute to their stone for man's body; that it worketh all contrary effects, but still to the good and benefit of nature. But yet, without praying in aid of alchymists, there is a manifest image of this in the ordinary course of nature. For in bodies, union strengtheneth and cherisheth any natural action; and, on the other side, weakeneth and dulleth any violent impression: and even so is it of minds.

The second fruit of friendship is healthful and sovereign for the understanding, as the first is for the affections. For friendship maketh indeed a fair day in the affections, from storm and tempests; but it maketh daylight in the understanding, out of darkness and confusion of thoughts. Neither is this to be understood only of faithful counsel, which a man receiveth from his friend; but before you come to that, certain it is that whosoever hath his mind fraught with many thoughts, his wits and understanding do clarify and break up, in the communicating and dis-coursing with another: he tosseth his thoughts more easily; he marshalleth them more orderly; he seeth how they look when they are turned into words; finally, he waxeth wiser than himself; and that more by an hour's discourse than by a day's meditation. It was well said by Themistocles to the king of Persia, *that speech was like cloth of Arras, opened and put abroad; whereby the imagery doth appear in figure; whereas in thoughts they lie but as in packs*. Neither is this second fruit of friendship, in opening the understanding, restrained only to such friends as are able to give a man counsel: (they indeed are best); but even without that, a man learneth of himself, and bringeth his own thoughts to light, and whetteth his wits as against a stone, which itself cuts not. In a word, a man were better relate himself to a statua or picture, than to suffer his thoughts to pass in smother.

Add now, to make this second fruit of friendship complete, that other point, which lieth more open, and falleth within vulgar observation; which is faithful counsel from a friend. Heraclitus saith well in one of his enigmas, *Dry light is ever the best*. And certain it is that the light that a man receiveth by counsel from another is drier and purer than that which cometh from his own understanding and judgement; which is ever infused and drenched in his affections and customs. So as there is as much difference between the counsel that a friend giveth, and that a man giveth himself, as there is between the counsel of a friend and of a flatterer. For there is no such flatterer as is a man's self; and there is no such remedy against flattery of a man's self as the liberty of a friend. Counsel is of two sorts; the one concerning manners, the other concerning business. For the first; the best preservative to keep the mind in health is the faithful admonition of a friend. The calling of a man's self to a strict account is a medicine, sometime, too piercing and corrosive. Reading good books of morality is a little flat and dead. Observing our faults in others is sometimes unproper for our case. But the best receipt (best, I say, to work, and best to take) is the admonition of a friend. It is a strange thing to behold what gross errors and extreme absurdities many (especially of the greater sort) do commit, for want of a friend to tell them of them, to the great damage both of their fame and fortune. For, as

Of Friendship

S. James saith, they are as men, *that look sometimes into a glass, and presently forget their own shape and favour.* As for business, a man may think, if he will, that two eyes see no more than one; or that a gamester seeth always more than a looker-on; or that a man in anger is as wise as he that hath said over the four and twenty letters; or that a musket may be shot off as well upon the arm as upon a rest; and such other fond and high imaginations, to think himself all in all. But when all is done, the help of good counsel is that which setteth business straight. And if any man think that he will take counsel, but it shall be by pieces; asking counsel in one business of one man, and in another business of another man; it is well (that is to say, better perhaps than if he asked none at all); but he runneth two dangers. One, that he shall not be faithfully counselled; for it is a rare thing, except it be from a perfect and entire friend, to have counsel given, but such as shall be bowed and crooked to some ends which he hath that giveth it. The other, that he shall have counsel given, hurtful and unsafe (though with good meaning), and mixed partly of mischief and partly of remedy: even as if you would call a physician, that is thought good for the cure of the disease you complain of, but is unacquainted with your body; and therefore may put you in way for a present cure, but overthroweth your health in some other kind; and so cure the disease and kill the patient. But a friend that is wholly acquainted with a man's estate will beware, by furthering any present business, how he dasheth upon other inconvenience. And therefore rest not upon scattered counsels; they will rather distract and mislead than settle and direct.

After these two noble fruits of friendship (peace in the affections, and support of the judgement) followeth the last fruit, which is like the pomegranate, full of many kernels; I mean aid and bearing a part in all actions and occasions. Here the best way to represent to life the manifold use of friendship is to cast and see how many things there are which a man cannot do

Essay XXVIII.—OF EXPENSE

RICHES are for spending, and spending for honour and good actions. Therefore extraordinary expense must be limited by the worth of the occasion; for voluntary undoing may be as well for a man's country as for the kingdom of heaven. But ordinary expense ought to be limited by a man's estate; and governed with such regard, as it be within his compass; and not subject to deceit and abuse of servants; and ordered to the best shew, that the bills may be less than the estimation abroad. Certainly, if a man will keep but of even hand, his ordinary expenses ought to be but to the half of his receipts; and if he think to wax rich, but to the third part. It is no baseness for the greatest to descend and look into their own estate. Some forbear it, not upon negligence alone, but doubting to bring themselves into melancholy, in respect they shall find it broken. But wounds cannot be cured without searching. He that cannot look into his own estate at all, had need both choose well those whom he employeth, and change them often; for new are more timorous and less subtile. He that can look into his estate but seldom, it behoveth him to turn all to certainties. A man had need, if he be plentiful in some kind of expense, to be as saving again in some other. As, if he be plentiful in diet, to be saving in apparel; if he be plentiful in the hall, to be saving in the stable; and the like. For he that is plentiful in expenses of all kinds will hardly be preserved from decay. In clearing of a man's estate, he may as well hurt himself in being too sudden, as in letting it run on too long. For hasty selling is commonly as disadvantageable as interest. Besides, he that clears at once will relapse; for finding himself out of straits, he will revert to his customs: but he that cleareth by degrees induceth a habit of frugality, and gaineth as

well upon his mind as upon his estate. Certainly, who
hath a state to repair may not despise small things: and
commonly it is less dishonourable to abridge petty
charges, than to stoop to petty gettings. A man ought
warily to begin charges which once begun will continue:
but in matters that return not he may be more magni-
ficent.

Bacon's Essays

The greatness of an estate in bulk and territory doth fall under measure; and the greatness of finances and revenue doth fall under computation. The population may appear by musters; and the number and greatness of cities and towns, by cards and maps. But yet there is not anything amongst civil affairs more subject to error, than the right valuation and true judgement concerning the power and forces of an estate. The kingdom of heaven is compared, not to any great kernel or nut, but to a grain of mustard-seed; which is one of the least grains, but hath in it a property and spirit hastily to get up and spread. So are there states great in territory, and yet not apt to enlarge or command; and some that have but a small dimension of stem, and yet apt to be the foundations of great monarchies.

Walled towns, stored arsenals and armouries, goodly races of horse, chariots of war, elephants, ordnance, artillery, and the like: all this is but a sheep in a lion's skin, except the breed and disposition of the people be stout and warlike. Nay, number (itself) in armies importeth not much, where the people is of weak courage; for (as Virgil saith) *It never troubles a wolf how many the sheep be.* The army of the Persians in the plains of Arbela was such a vast sea of people, as it did somewhat astonish the commanders in Alexander's army; who came to him therefore, and wished him to set upon them by night; but he answered, *He would not pilfer the victory.* And the defeat was easy. When Tigranes the Armenian, being encamped upon a hill with 400,000 men, discovered the army of the Romans, being not above 14,000, marching towards him, he made himself merry with it and said, *Yonder men are too many for an ambassage and too few for a fight.* But before the sun set, he found them enough to give him the chase with infinite slaughter. Many are the examples of the great odds between number and courage: so that a man may truly make a judgement, that the principal point of greatness in any state is to have a race of military men. Neither is money the sinews of war (as it is trivially said), where the sinews of men's arms, in base and effeminate people, are failing. For Solon said well to Crœsus (when in ostentation he shewed him his gold), *Sir, if any other come that hath better iron than you, he will be master of all this gold.* Therefore let any prince or state think soberly of his forces, except his militia of natives be of good and valiant soldiers. And let princes, on the other side, that have subjects of martial disposition, know their own strength; unless they be otherwise wanting unto themselves. As for mercenary forces (which is the help in this case), all examples shew, that, whatsoever estate or prince doth rest upon them, *he may spread his feathers for a time, but he will mew them soon after.*

The blessing of Judah and Issachar will never meet; *that the same people or nation should be both the lion's whelp and the ass between burthens :* neither will it be, that a people overlaid with taxes should ever become valiant and martial. It is true that taxes levied by consent of the estate do abate men's courage less: as it hath been seen notably in the excises of the Low Countries; and, in some degree, in the subsidies of England. For you must note that we speak now of the heart and not of the purse. So that although the same tribute and tax, laid by consent or by imposing, be all one to the purse, yet it works diversely upon the courage. So that you may conclude, *that no people overcharged with tribute is fit for empire.*

Let states that aim at greatness take heed how their nobility and gentlemen do multiply too fast. For that maketh the common subject grow to be a peasant and base swain, driven out of heart, and in effect but the gentleman's labourer. Even as you may see in coppice woods; if you leave your staddles too thick, you shall never have clean underwood, but shrubs and bushes. So in countries, if the gentlemen be too many, the commons will be base; and you will bring it to that, that not the hundred poll will be fit for an helmet; especially as to the infantry, which is the nerve of an army; and so there will be great population and little strength. This which I speak of hath been no where better seen than by comparing of England and France; whereof England, though far less in territory and population, hath been (nevertheless) an over-match; in regard the middle people of England make good soldiers, which the peasants of France do not. And herein the device of King Henry the Seventh (whereof I have spoken largely in the *History of his Life*) was profound and admirable; in making farms and houses of husbandry of a standard; that is, maintained with such a proportion of land unto them, as may breed a subject to live in convenient plenty and no servile condition; and to keep the plough in the hands of the owners, and not mere hirelings. And thus indeed you shall attain to Virgil's character, which he gives to ancient Italy:

—Terra potens armis atque ubere glebæ.

Neither is that state (which, for any thing I know, is almost peculiar to England, and hardly to be found any where else, except it be perhaps in Poland) to be passed over; I mean the state of free servants and attendants upon noblemen and gentlemen; which are no ways inferior unto the yeomanry for arms. And therefore, out of all question, the splendour and magnificence and great retinues and hospitality of noblemen and gentlemen, received into custom, doth much conduce unto martial greatness. Whereas, contrariwise, the close and reserved living of noblemen and gentlemen causeth a penury of military forces.

By all means it is to be procured, that the trunk of Nebuchadnezzar's tree of monarchy be great enough to bear the branches and the boughs; that is, that the natural subjects of the crown or state bear a sufficient proportion to the stranger subjects that they govern. Therefore all states that are liberal of naturalization towards strangers are fit for empire. For to think that an handful of people can, with the greatest courage and policy in the world, embrace too large extent of dominion, it may hold for a time, but it will fail suddenly. The Spartans were a nice people in point of naturalization;

whereby, while they kept their compass, they stood firm; but when they did spread, and their boughs were becomen too great for their stem, they became a windfall upon the sudden. Never any state was in this point so open to receive strangers into their body as were the Romans. Therefore it sorted with them accordingly; for they grew to the greatest monarchy. Their manner was to grant naturalization (which they cal¹ed *jus civitatis*), and to grant it in the highest degree; that is, not only *jus commercii, jus connubii, jus hæreditatis,* but also *jus suffragii* and *jus honorum.* And this, not to singular persons alone, but likewise to whole families; yea, to cities, and sometimes to nations. Add to this their custom of plantation of colonies, whereby the Roman plant was removed into the soil of other nations. And putting both constitutions together, you will say that it was not the Romans that spread upon the world, but it was the world that spread upon the Romans; and that was the sure way of greatness. I have marvelled sometimes at Spain, how they clasp and contain so large dominions with so few natural Spaniards: but sure the whole compass of Spain is a very great body of a tree; far above Rome and Sparta at the first. And besides, though they have not had that usage to naturalize liberally, yet they have that which is next to it; that is, to employ almost indifferently all nations in their militia of ordinary soldiers; yea, and sometimes in their highest commands. Nay, it seemeth at this instant they are sensible of this want of natives; as by the Pragmatical Sanction, now published, appeareth.

It is certain, that sedentary and within-door arts and delicate manufacturers (that require rather the finger than the arm) have in their nature a contrariety to a military disposition. And generally all warlike people are a little idle, and love danger better than travail; neither must they be too much broken of it, if they shall be preserved in vigour. Therefore it was great advantage, in the ancient states of Sparta, Athens, Rome, and others, that they had the use of slaves, which commonly did rid those manufactures. But

that is abolished, in greatest part, by the Christian law.
That which cometh nearest to it is to leave those arts
chiefly to strangers (which for that purpose are the
more easily to be received), and to contain the principal
bulk of the vulgar natives within those three kinds:
tillers of the ground; free servants; and handicraftsmen
of strong and manly arts, as smiths, masons, carpenters,
etc.; not reckoning professed soldiers.

But above all, for empire and greatness, it importeth
most, that a nation do profess arms as their principal
honour, study, and occupation. For the things which
we formerly have spoken of are but habilitations towards
arms; and what is habilitation without intention and
act? Romulus, after his death (as they report or feign),
sent a present to the Romans, that above all they should
intend arms, and then they should prove the greatest
empire of the world. The fabric of the state of Sparta
was wholly (though not wisely) framed and composed
to that scope and end. The Persians and Macedonians
had it for a flash. The Gauls, Germans, Goths, Saxons,
Normans, and others, had it for a time. The Turks
have it at this day, though in great declination. Of
Christian Europe, they that have it are, in effect, only
the Spaniards. But it is so plain, *that every man
profiteth in that he most intendeth*, that it needeth not to
be stood upon. It is enough to point at it; that no
nation, which doth not directly profess arms, may look
to have greatness fall into their mouths. And, on the
other side, it is a most certain oracle of time, that those
states that continue long in that profession (as the
Romans and Turks principally have done) do wonders.
And those that have professed arms but for an age have
notwithstanding commonly attained that greatness in
that age which maintained them long after, when their
profession and exercise of arms hath grown to decay.

Incident to this point is, for a state to have those
laws or customs which may reach forth unto them just
occasions (as may be pretended) of war. For there is
that justice imprinted in the nature of men, that they
enter not upon wars (whereof so many calamities do

ensue) but upon some, at the least specious, grounds
and quarrels. The Turk hath at hand, for cause of war,
the propagation of his law or sect; a quarrel that he
may always command. The Romans, though they
esteemed the extending the limits of their empire to be
great honour to their generals when it was done, yet
they never rested upon that alone to begin a war. First,
therefore, let nations that pretend to greatness have
this: that they be sensible of wrongs, either upon
borderers, merchants, or politic ministers; and that they
sit not too long upon a provocation. Secondly, let
them be prest and ready to give aids and succours to
their confederates: as it ever was with the Romans;
insomuch as if the confederate had leagues defensive
with divers other states, and, upon invasion offered, did
implore their aids severally, yet the Romans would ever
be the foremost, and leave it to none other to have the
honour. As for the wars which were anciently made on
the behalf of a kind of party, or tacit conformity of
estate, I do not see how they may be well justified: as
when the Romans made a war for the liberty of Græcia;
or when the Lacedæmonians and Athenians made wars
to set up or pull down democracies and oligarchies; or
when wars were made by foreigners, under the pretence
of justice or protection, to deliver the subjects of others
from tyranny and oppression; and the like. Let it
suffice, that no estate expect to be great, that is not
awake upon any just occasion of arming.

No body can be healthful without exercise, neither
natural body nor politic; and certainly, to a kingdom or
estate, a just and honourable war is the true exercise.
A civil war, indeed, is like the heat of a fever; but a
foreign war is like the heat of exercise, and serveth to
keep the body in health; for in a slothful peace, both
courages will effeminate and manners corrupt. But
howsoever it be for happiness, without all question for
greatness it maketh to be still for the most part in arms;
and the strength of a veteran army (though it be a
chargeable business), always on foot, is that which
commonly giveth the law, or at least the reputation,

amongst all neighbour states; as may well be seen in Spain, which hath had, in one part or other, a veteran army, almost continually, now by the space of six-score years.

To be master of the sea is an abridgement of a monarchy. Cicero, writing to Atticus, of Pompey his preparation against Cæsar, saith: *Consilium Pompeii plane Themistocleum est ; putat enim, qui mari potitur, eum rerum potiri*. And, without doubt, Pompey had tired out Cæsar, if upon vain confidence he had not left that way. We see the great effects of battles by sea. The battle of Actium decided the empire of the world. The battle of Lepanto arrested the greatness of the Turk. There be many examples where sea-fights have been final to the war; but this is when princes or states have set up their rest upon the battles. But thus much is certain, that he that commands the sea is at great liberty, and may take as much and as little of the war as he will. Whereas those that be strongest by land are many times nevertheless in great straits. Surely, at this day, with us of Europe, the vantage of strength at sea (which is one of the principal dowries of this kingdom of Great Britain) is great: both because most of the kingdoms of Europe are not merely inland, but girt with the sea most part of their compass; and because the wealth of both Indies seems in great part but an accessary to the command of the seas.

The wars of latter ages seem to be made in the dark, in respect of the glory and honour which reflected upon men from the wars in ancient time. There be now, for martial encouragement, some degrees and orders of chivalry, which nevertheless are conferred promiscuously upon soldiers and no soldiers; and some remembrance perhaps upon the scutcheon; and some hospitals for maimed soldiers; and such like things. But in ancient times, the trophies erected upon the place of the victory; the funeral laudatives and monuments for those that died in the wars; the crowns and garlands personal; the style of Emperor, which the great kings of the world after borrowed; the triumphs of the generals upon their return; the great donatives and largesses upon the disbanding of the armies; were things able to inflame all men's courages. But above all, that of the triumph, amongst the Romans, was not pageants or gaudery, but one of the wisest and noblest institutions that ever was. For it contained three things: honour to the general; riches to the treasury out of the spoils; and donatives to the army. But that honour perhaps were not fit for monarchies, except it be in the person of the monarch himself, or his sons; as it came to pass in the times of the Roman emperors, who did impropriate the actual triumphs to themselves and their sons, for such wars as they did achieve in person, and left only, for wars achieved by subjects, some triumphal garments and ensigns to the general.

To conclude: no man can by *care taking* (as the Scripture saith) *add a cubit to his stature*, in this little model of a man's body: but in the great frame of kingdoms and commonwealths, it is in the power of princes or estates to add amplitude and greatness to their kingdoms. For by introducing such ordinances, constitutions, and customs, as we have now touched, they may sow greatness to their posterity and succession. But these things are commonly not observed, but left to take their chance.

Essay XXX.—OF REGIMENT OF HEALTH

THERE is a wisdom in this beyond the rules of physic: a man's own observation, what he finds good of, and what he finds hurt of, is the best physic to preserve health. But it is a safer conclusion to say, *This agreeth not well with me, therefore I will not continue it,* than this, *I find no offence of this, therefore I may use it.* For strength of nature in youth passeth over many excesses, which are owing a man till his age. Discern of the coming on of years, and think not to do the same things still; for age will not be defied. Beware of sudden change in any great point of diet, and if necessity enforce it, fit the rest to it. For it is a secret, both in nature and state, that it is safer to change many things than one. Examine thy customs of diet, sleep, exercise, apparel, and the like; and try, in any thing thou shalt judge hurtful, to discontinue it by little and little; but so as, if thou dost find any inconvenience by the change, thou come back to it again: for it is hard to distinguish that which is generally held good and wholesome, from that which is good particularly, and fit for thine own body. To be free-minded and cheerfully disposed at hours of meat and of sleep and of exercise, is one of the best precepts of long lasting. As for the passions and studies of the mind; avoid envy; anxious fears; anger fretting inwards; subtile and knotty inquisitions; joys and exhilarations in excess; sadness not communicated. Entertain hopes; mirth rather than joy; variety of delights, rather than surfeit of them; wonder and admiration, and therefore novelties; studies that fill the mind with splendid and illustrious objects, as histories, fables, and contemplations of nature. If you fly physic in health altogether, it will be too strange for your body when you shall need it. If

Of Regiment of Health

you make it too familiar, it will work no extraordinary effect when sickness cometh. I commend rather some diet for certain seasons, than frequent use of physic, except it be grown into a custom. For those diets alter the body more, and trouble it less. Despise no new accident in your body, but ask opinion of it. In sickness, respect health principally; and in health, action. For those that put their bodies to endure in health, may, in most sicknesses which are not very sharp, be cured only with diet and tendering. Celsus could never have spoken it as a physician, had he not been a wise man withal, when he giveth it for one of the great precepts of health and lasting, that a man do vary and interchange contraries, but with an inclination to the more benign extreme: use fasting and full eating, but rather full eating; watching and sleep, but rather sleep; sitting and exercise, but rather exercise; and the like. So shall nature be cherished, and yet taught masteries. Physicians are some of them so pleasing and conformable to the humour of the patient, as they press not the true cure of the disease; and some other are so regular in proceeding according to art for the disease, as they respect not sufficiently the condition of the patient. Take one of a middle temper; or if it may not be found in one man, combine two of either sort; and forget not to call as well the best acquainted with your body, as the best reputed of for his faculty.

Essay XXXI.—OF SUSPICION

Suspicions amongst thoughts are like bats amongst birds, they ever fly by twilight. Certainly they are to be repressed, or at the least well guarded: for they cloud the mind; they leese friends; and they check with business, whereby business cannot go on currently and constantly. They dispose kings to tyranny, husbands to jealousy, wise men to irresolution and melancholy. They are defects, not in the heart, but in the brain; for they take place in the stoutest natures: as in the example of Henry the Seventh of England: there was not a more suspicious man, nor a more stout. And in such a composition they do small hurt. For commonly they are not admitted but with examination, whether they be likely or no? But in fearful natures they gain ground too fast. There is nothing makes a man suspect much, more than to know little; and therefore men should remedy suspicion by procuring to know more, and not to keep their suspicions in smother. What would men have? Do they think those they employ and deal with are saints? Do they not think they will have their own ends, and be truer to themselves than to them? Therefore there is no better way to moderate suspicions, than to account upon such suspicions as true, and yet to bridle them as false. For so far a man ought to make use of suspicions, as to provide as, if that should be true that he suspects, yet it may do him no hurt. Suspicions, that the mind of itself gathers, are but buzzes; but suspicions, that are artificially nourished and put into men's heads by the tales and whisperings of others, have stings. Certainly, the best mean to clear the way in this same wood of suspicions, is frankly to communicate them with the party that he suspects: for thereby he shall be sure to know more of the truth

Of Suspicion

of them than he did before; and withal shall make that party more circumspect not to give further cause of suspicion. But this would not be done to men of base natures; for they, if they find themselves once suspected, will never be true. The Italian says, *Sospetto licentia fede;* as if suspicion did give a passport to faith: but it ought rather to kindle it to discharge itself.

Essay XXXII.—OF DISCOURSE

Some in their discourse desire rather commendation of wit, in being able to hold all arguments, than of judgement, in discerning what is true; as if it were a praise to know what might be said, and not what should be thought. Some have certain common places and themes wherein they are good, and want variety; which kind of poverty is for the most part tedious, and, when it is once perceived, ridiculous. The honourablest part of talk is to give the occasion; and again to moderate and pass to somewhat else; for then a man leads the dance. It is good, in discourse, and speech of conversation, to vary and intermingle speech of the present occasion with arguments; tales with reasons; asking of questions with telling of opinions; and jest with earnest: for it is a dull thing to tire, and, as we say now, to jade any thing too far. As for jest, there be certain things which ought to be privileged from it; namely, religion, matters of state, great persons, any man's present business of importance, and any case that deserveth pity. Yet there be some that think their wits have been asleep, except they dart out somewhat that is piquant and to the quick: that is a vein which would be bridled:

Parce, puer, stimulis, et fortius utere loris.

And generally, men ought to find the difference between saltness and bitterness. Certainly, he that hath a satirical vein, as he maketh others afraid of his wit, so he had need be afraid of others' memory. He that questioneth much, shall learn much, and content much; but especially if he apply his questions to the skill of the persons whom he asketh: for he shall give them occasion to please themselves in speaking, and himself shall continually gather knowledge. But let his ques-

tions not be troublesome; for that is fit for a poser.
And let him be sure to leave other men their turns to
speak. Nay, if there be any that would reign and take
up all the time, let him find means to take them off and
to bring others on; as musicians use to do with those
that dance too long galliards. If you dissemble sometimes your knowledge of that you are thought to know,
you shall be thought another time to know that you
know not. Speech of a man's self ought to be seldom,
and well chosen. I knew one was wont to say in scorn,
He must needs be a wise man, he speaks so much of himself :
and there is but one case wherein a man may commend
himself with good grace, and that is in commending
virtue in another, especially if it be such a virtue whereunto himself pretendeth. Speech of touch towards
others should be sparingly used; for discourse ought to
be as a field, without coming home to any man. I
knew two noblemen, of the west part of England,
whereof the one was given to scoff, but kept ever royal
cheer in his house: the other would ask of those that
had been at the other's table, *Tell truly, was there never
a flout or dry blow given ?* to which the guest would
answer, *Such and such a thing passed :* the lord would
say, *I thought he would mar a good dinner.* Discretion
of speech is more than eloquence; and to speak
agreeably to him with whom we deal, is more than to
speak in good words or in good order. A good continued speech, without a good speech of interlocution,
shews slowness; and a good reply or second speech,
without a good settled speech, sheweth shallowness and
weakness. As we see in beasts, that those that are
weakest in the course, are yet nimblest in the turn; as it
is betwixt the greyhound and the hare. To use too
many circumstances, ere one come to the matter, is
wearisome; to use none at all, is blunt.

Essay XXXIII.—OF PLANTATIONS

PLANTATIONS are amongst ancient, primitive, and heroical works. When the world was young, it begat more children; but now it is old, it begets fewer: for I may justly account new plantations to be the children of former kingdoms. I like a plantation in a pure soil; that is, where people are not displanted to the end to plant in others. For else it is rather an extirpation than a plantation. Planting of countries is like planting of woods; for you must make account to leese almost twenty years' profit, and expect your recompense in the end. For the principal thing that hath been the destruction of most plantations, hath been the base and hasty drawing of profit in the first years. It is true, speedy profit is not to be neglected, as far as may stand with the good of the plantation, but no further. It is a shameful and unblessed thing to take the scum of people, and wicked condemned men, to be the people with whom you plant: and not only so, but it spoileth the plantation; for they will ever live like rogues, and not fall to work, but be lazy, and do mischief, and spend victuals, and be quickly weary, and then certify over to their country to the discredit of the plantation. The people wherewith you plant ought to be gardeners, ploughmen, labourers, smiths, carpenters, joiners, fishermen, fowlers, with some few apothecaries, surgeons, cooks, and bakers. In a country of plantation, first look about, what kind of victual the country yields of itself to hand; as chestnuts, walnuts, pine-apples, olives, dates, plums, cherries, wild honey, and the like; and make use of them. Then consider what victual or esculent things there are, which grow speedily, and within the year; as parsnips, carrots, turnips, onions, radish, artichokes of Hierusalem, maize, and the like. For wheat, barley, and oats, they ask too much labour; but with peas and beans you may begin, both because they ask less labour, and because they serve for meat as well as for bread. And of rice likewise cometh a great increase, and it is a kind of meat. Above all, there ought to be brought store of biscuit, oat-meal, flour, meal, and the like, in the beginning, till bread may be had. For beasts or birds, take chiefly such as are least subject to diseases, and multiply fastest; as swine, goats, cocks, hens, turkeys, geese, house-doves, and the like. The victual in plantations ought to be expended almost as in a besieged town; that is, with certain allowance. And let the main part of the ground employed to gardens or corn be to a common stock; and to be laid in, and stored up, and then delivered out in proportion; besides some spots of ground that any particular person will manure for his own private. Consider likewise what commodities the soil where the plantation is doth naturally yield, that they may some way help to defray the charge of the plantation: so it be not, as was said, to the untimely prejudice of the main business; as it hath fared with tobacco in Virginia. Wood commonly aboundeth but too much; and therefore timber is fit to be one. If there be iron ore, and streams whereupon to set the mills, iron is a brave commodity where wood aboundeth. Making of bay-salt, if the climate be proper for it, would be put in experience. Growing silk likewise, if any be, is a likely commodity. Pitch and tar, where store of firs and pines are, will not fail. So drugs and sweet woods, where they are, cannot but yield great profit. Soap-ashes likewise, and other things that may be thought of. But moil not too much under ground; for the hope of mines is very uncertain, and useth to make the planters lazy in other things. For government, let it be in the hands of one, assisted with some counsel; and let them have a commission to exercise martial laws, with some limitation. And above all, let men make that profit of being in the wilderness, as they have God always, and His service, before their eyes. Let not the government of the plantation depend upon too many counsellors and undertakers in the country that inheritance, testaments, and the like), they come tumbling upon a man. But it mought be applied likewise to Pluto, taking him for the devil. For when riches come from the devil (as by fraud and oppression and unjust means), they come upon speed. The ways to enrich are many, and most of them foul. Parsimony is one of the best, and yet is not innocent; for it withholdeth men from works of liberality and charity. The improvement of the ground is the most natural obtaining of riches; for it is our great mother's blessing, the earth's; but it is slow. And yet, where men of great wealth do stoop to husbandry, it multiplieth riches exceedingly. I knew a nobleman in England, that had the greatest audits of any man in my time: a great grazier, a great sheep-master, a great timber man, a great collier, a great corn-master, a great lead-man, and so of iron, and a number of the like points of husbandry: so as the earth seemed a sea to him, in respect of the perpetual importation. It was truly observed by one, that himself came very hardly to a little riches, and very easily to great riches. For when a man's stock is come to that, that he can expect the prime of markets, and overcome those bargains which for their greatness are few men's money, and be partner in the industries of younger men, he cannot but increase mainly. The gains of ordinary trades and vocations are honest, and furthered by two things chiefly: by diligence, and by a good name for good and fair dealing. But the gains of bargains are of a more doubtful nature; when men shall wait upon others' necessity, broke by servants and instruments to draw them on, put off others cunningly that would be better chapmen, and the like practices, which are crafty and naught. As for the chopping of bargains, when a man buys, not to hold, but to sell over again, that commonly grindeth double, both upon the seller and upon the buyer. Sharings do greatly enrich, if the hands be well chosen that are trusted. Usury is the certainest means of gain, though one of the worst; as that whereby a man doth eat his bread *in sudore vultûs alieni*, and besides, doth plough upon Sundays. But yet, certain

Of Riches

though it be, it hath flaws; for that the scriveners and brokers do value unsound men, to serve their own turn. The fortune in being the first in an invention, or in a privilege, doth cause sometimes a wonderful overgrowth in riches; as it was with the first sugar man in the Canaries: therefore if a man can play the true logician, to have as well judgement as invention, he may do great matters; especially if the times be fit. He that resteth upon gains certain, shall hardly grow to great riches: and he that puts all upon adventures, doth oftentimes break and come to poverty: it is good therefore to guard adventures with certainties that may uphold losses. Monopolies, and coemption of wares for re-sale, where they are not restrained, are great means to enrich; especially if the party have intelligence what things are like to come into request, and so store himself beforehand. Riches gotten by service, though it be of the best rise, yet when they are gotten by flattery, feeding humours, and other servile conditions, they may be placed amongst the worst. As for fishing for testaments and executorships (as Tacitus saith of Seneca, *testamenta et orbos tanquam indagine capi*) it is yet worse; by how much men submit themselves to meaner persons than in service. Believe not much them that seem to despise riches; for they despise them that despair of them; and none worse, when they come to them. Be not pennywise; riches have wings, and sometimes they fly away of themselves, sometimes they must be set flying to bring in more. Men leave their riches either to their kindred, or to the public; and moderate portions prosper best in both. A great state left to an heir, is as a lure to all the birds of prey round about to seize on him, if he be not the better stablished in years and judgement. Likewise glorious gifts and foundations are like *sacrifices without salt;* and but the painted sepulchres of alms, which soon will putrefy and corrupt inwardly. Therefore measure not thine advancements by quantity, but frame them by measure: and defer not charities till death; for certainly, if a man weigh it rightly, he that doth so is rather liberal of another man's than of his own.

Of Prophecies

expounds it of Vespasian. Domitian dreamed, the
night before he was slain, that a golden head was growing out of the nape of his neck: and indeed the succession that followed him, for many years, made golden
times. Henry the Sixth of England said of Henry the
Seventh, when he was a lad, and gave him water: *This
is the lad that shall enjoy the crown for which we strive.*
When I was in France, I heard from one Dr. Pena, that
the Q. Mother, who was given to curious arts, caused
the King her husband's nativity to be calculated, under
a false name; and the astrologer gave a judgement, that
he should be killed in a duel; at which the Queen
laughed, thinking her husband to be above challenges
and duels: but he was slain upon a course at tilt, the
splinters of the staff of Montgomery going in at his
beaver. The trivial prophecy which I heard, when I
was a child, and Queen Elizabeth was in the flower of
her years, was:

> *When Hempe is sponne,*
> *England's done.*

Whereby it was generally conceived that after the
princes had reigned which had the principal letters of
that word *hempe* (which were Henry, Edward, Mary,
Philip, and Elizabeth), England should come to utter
confusion: which, thanks be to God, is verified only in
the change of the name; for that the King's style is
now no more of England, but of Britain. There was
also another prophecy, before the year of 88, which I do
not well understand:

> *There shall be seene upon a day,*
> *Betweene the Baugh and the May,*
> *The Blacke Fleet of Norway.*
> *When that that is come and gone,*
> *England build Houses of Lime and Stone,*
> *For after Warres shall you have None.*

It was generally conceived to be meant of the Spanish
fleet, that came in 88: for that the king of Spain's sur-

name, as they say, is *Norway*. The prediction of Regiomontanus,

Octogesimus octavus mirabilis annus,

was thought likewise accomplished in the sending of that great fleet, being the greatest in strength, though not in number, of all that ever swam upon the sea. As for Cleon's dream, I think it was a jest. It was, that he was devoured of a long dragon; and it was expounded of a maker of sausages, that troubled him exceedingly. There are numbers of the like kind; especially if you include dreams, and predictions of astrology. But I have set down these few only of certain credit, for example. My judgement is, that they ought all to be despised; and ought to serve but for winter talk by the fire-side. Though when I say despised, I mean it as for belief; for otherwise, the spreading or publishing of them is in no sort to be despised. For they have done much mischief; and I see many severe laws made to suppress them. That that hath given them grace, and some credit, consisteth in three things. First, that men mark when they hit, and never mark when they miss; as they do generally also of dreams. The second is, that probable conjectures, or obscure traditions, many times turn themselves into prophecies; while the nature of man, which coveteth divination, thinks it no peril to foretell that which indeed they do but collect. As that of Seneca's verse. For so much was then subject to demonstration, that the globe of the earth had great parts beyond the Atlantic; which mought be probably conceived not to be all sea: and adding thereto the tradition in Plato's *Timæus*, and his *Atlanticus* it mought encourage one to turn it to a prediction. The third and last (which is the great one) is, that almost all of them, being infinite in number, have been impostures, and by idle and crafty brains merely contrived and feigned after the event past.

Essay XXXVI.—OF AMBITION

AMBITION is like choler; which is an humour that maketh men active, earnest, full of alacrity, and stirring, if it be not stopped. But if it be stopped, and cannot have his way, it becometh adust, and thereby malign and venomous. So ambitious men, if they find the way open for their rising, and still get forward, they are rather busy than dangerous; but if they be checked in their desires, they become secretly discontent, and look upon men and matters with an evil eye, and are best pleased when things go backward; which is the worst property in a servant of a prince or state. Therefore it is good for princes, if they use ambitious men, to handle it so as they be still progressive and not retrograde: which because it cannot be without inconvenience, it is good not to use such natures at all. For if they rise not with their service, they will take order to make their service fall with them. But since we have said it were good not to use men of ambitious natures, except it be upon necessity, it is fit we speak in what cases they are of necessity. Good commanders in the wars must be taken, be they never so ambitious: for the use of their service dispenseth with the rest; and to take a soldier without ambition is to pull off his spurs. There is also great use of ambitious men in being screens to princes in matters of danger and envy: for no man will take that part, except he be like a seeled dove, that mounts and mounts because he cannot see about him. There is use also of ambitious men in pulling down the greatness of any subject that overtops: as Tiberius used Macro in the pulling down of Sejanus. Since therefore they must be used in such cases, there resteth to speak how they are to be bridled, that they may be less dangerous. There is less danger of them if they be of mean birth, than if they be noble; and if they be rather harsh of nature, than gracious and popular; and if they be rather new raised, than grown cunning and fortified in their greatness. It is counted by some a weakness in princes to have favourites; but it is of all others the best remedy against ambitious great-ones. For when the way of pleasuring and displeasuring lieth by the favourite, it is impossible any other should be over-great. Another means to curb them, is to balance them by others as proud as they. But then there must be some middle counsellors, to keep things steady; for without that ballast the ship will roll too much. At the least, a prince may animate and inure some meaner persons to be, as it were, scourges to ambitious men. As for the having of them obnoxious to ruin, if they be of fearful natures, it may do well; but if they be stout and daring, it may precipitate their designs, and prove dangerous. As for the pulling of them down, if the affairs require it, and that it may not be done with safety suddenly, the only way is the interchange continually of favours and disgraces; whereby they may not know what to expect, and be, as it were, in a wood. Of ambitions, it is less harmful, the ambition to prevail in great things, than that other, to appear in every thing; for that breeds confusion, and mars business. But yet it is less danger to have an ambitious man stirring in business, than great in dependences. He that seeketh to be eminent amongst able men hath a great task; but that is ever good for the public. But he that plots to be the only figure amongst cyphers is the decay of an whole age. Honour hath three things in it: the vantage ground to do good; the approach to kings and principal persons; and the raising of a man's own fortunes. He that hath the best of these intentions, when he aspireth, is an honest man; and that prince that can discern of these intentions in another that aspireth, is a wise prince. Generally, let princes and states choose such ministers as are more sensible of duty than of rising; and such as love business rather upon conscience than upon bravery: and let them discern a busy nature from a willing mind.

Essay XXXVII.—OF MASQUES AND TRIUMPHS

THESE things are but toys, to come amongst such serious observations. But yet, since princes will have such things, it is better they should be graced with elegancy, than daubed with cost. Dancing to song is a thing of great state and pleasure. I understand it, that the song be in quire, placed aloft, and accompanied with some broken music; and the ditty fitted to the device. Acting in song, especially in dialogues, hath an extreme good grace: I say acting, not dancing (for that is a mean and vulgar thing); and the voices of the dialogue would be strong and manly (a bass and a tenor, no treble); and the ditty high and tragical, not nice or dainty. Several quires, placed one over against another, and taking the voice by catches, anthem-wise, give great pleasure. Turning dances into figure is a childish curiosity. And generally, let it be noted, that those things which I here set down are such as do naturally take the sense, and not respect petty wonderments. It is true, the alterations of scenes, so it be quietly and without noise, are things of great beauty and pleasure; for they feed and relieve the eye, before it be full of the same object. Let the scenes abound with light, specially coloured and varied; and let the masquers, or any other, that are to come down from the scene, have some motions upon the scene itself before their coming down; for it draws the eye strangely, and makes it with great pleasure to desire to see that it cannot perfectly discern. Let the songs be loud and cheerful, and not chirpings or pulings. Let the music likewise be sharp and loud and well placed. The colours that shew best by candle-light are white, carnation, and a kind of sea-water-green; and oes, or spangs, as they are of no great cost, so they are of most glory. As for rich embroidery, it is lost and not discerned. Let the suits of the masquers be graceful, and such as become the person when the vizars are off: not after examples of known attires; Turks, soldiers, mariners, and the like. Let antimasques not be long; they have been commonly of fools, satyrs, baboons, wild-men, antics, beasts, sprites, witches, Ethiopes, pigmies, turquets, nymphs, rustics, Cupids, statuas moving, and the like. As for angels, it is not comical enough to put them in antimasques; and any thing that is hideous, as devils, giants, is on the other side as unfit. But chiefly, let the music of them be recreative, and with some strange changes. Some sweet odours, suddenly coming forth, without any drops falling, are, in such a company as there is steam and heat, things of great pleasure and refreshment. Double masques, one of men, another of ladies, addeth state and variety. But all is nothing, except the room be kept clear and neat.

For justs, and tourneys, and barriers; the glories of them are chiefly in the chariots, wherein the challengers make their entry; especially if they be drawn with strange beasts, as lions, bears, camels, and the like; or in the devices of their entrance; or in the bravery of their liveries; or in the goodly furniture of their horses and armour. But enough of these toys.

Essay XXXVIII.—OF NATURE IN MEN

NATURE is often hidden, sometimes overcome, seldom extinguished. Force maketh nature more violent in the return; doctrine and discourse maketh nature less importune; but custom only doth alter and subdue nature. He that seeketh victory over his nature, let him not set himself too great nor too small tasks: for the first will make him dejected by often failings; and the second will make him a small proceeder, though by often prevailings. And at the first let him practise with helps, as swimmers do with bladders or rushes; but after a time let him practise with disadvantages, as dancers do with thick shoes. For it breeds great perfection, if the practice be harder than the use. Where nature is mighty, and therefore the victory hard, the degrees had need be: first, to stay and arrest nature in time; like to him that would say over the four and twenty letters when he was angry: then, to go less in quantity; as if one should, in forbearing wine, come from drinking healths to a draught at a meal: and lastly, to discontinue altogether. But if a man have the fortitude and resolution to enfranchise himself at once, that is the best:

> *Optimus ille animi vindex lædentia pectus*
> *Vincula qui rupit, dedoluitque semel.*

Neither is the ancient rule amiss, to bend nature as a wand to a contrary extreme, whereby to set it right; understanding it, where the contrary extreme is no vice. Let not a man force a habit upon himself with a perpetual continuance, but with some intermission. For both the pause reinforceth the new onset; and if a man that is not perfect be ever in practice, he shall as well practise his errors as his abilities, and induce one habit of both; and there is no means to help this but by seasonable intermissions. But let not a man trust his victory over his nature too far; for nature will lay buried a great time, and yet revive upon the occasion or temptation. Like as it was with Æsop's damosel, turned from a cat to a woman; who sate very demurely at the board's end, till a mouse ran before her. Therefore let a man either avoid the occasion altogether; or put himself often to it, that he may be little moved with it. A man's nature is best perceived in privateness, for there is no affectation; in passion, for that putteth a man out of his precepts; and in a new case or experiment, for there custom leaveth him. They are happy men, whose natures sort with their vocations; otherwise they may say, *Multum incola fuit anima mea*, when they converse in those things they do not affect. In studies, whatsoever a man commandeth upon himself, let him set hours for it; but whatsoever is agreeable to his nature, let him take no care for any set times; for his thoughts will fly to it of themselves, so as the spaces of other business or studies will suffice. A man's nature runs either to herbs or weeds; therefore let him seasonably water the one, and destroy the other.

Essay XXXIX.—OF CUSTOM AND EDUCATION

MEN'S thoughts are much according to their inclination; their discourse and speeches according to their learning and infused opinions; but their deeds are after as they have been accustomed. And therefore, as Machiavel well noteth (though in an evil-favoured instance), there is no trusting to the force of nature nor to the bravery of words, except it be corroborate by custom. His instance is, that for the achieving of a desperate conspiracy, a man should not rest upon the fierceness of any man's nature, or his resolute undertakings; but take such an one as hath had his hands formerly in blood. But Machiavel knew not of a Friar Clement, nor a Ravillac, nor a Jaureguy, nor a Baltazar Gerard: yet his rule holdeth still, that nature, nor the engagement of words, are not so forcible as custom. Only superstition is now so well advanced, that men of the first blood are as firm as butchers by occupation; and votary resolution is made equipollent to custom, even in matter of blood. In other things, the predominancy of custom is every where visible; insomuch as a man would wonder to hear men profess, protest, engage, give great words, and then do just as they have done before; as if they were dead images and engines moved only by the wheels of custom. We see also the reign or tyranny of custom, what it is. The Indians (I mean the sect of their wise men) lay themselves quietly upon a stack of wood, and so sacrifice themselves by fire. Nay, the wives strive to be burned with the corpses of their husbands. The lads of Sparta, of ancient time, were wont to be scourged upon the altar of Diana, without so much as queching. I remember, in the beginning of Queen Elizabeth's time of England, an Irish rebel condemned put up a petition to the deputy, that he might be hanged in a with and not in an halter, because it had been so used with former rebels. There be monks in Russia, for penance, that will sit a whole night in a vessel of water, till they be engaged with hard ice. Many examples may be put of the force of custom, both upon mind and body. Therefore, since custom is the principal magistrate of man's life, let men by all means endeavour to obtain good customs. Certainly, custom is most perfect when it beginneth in young years: this we call education; which is, in effect, but an early custom. So we see, in languages the tongue is more pliant to all expressions and sounds, the joints are more supple to all feats of activity and motions, in youth than afterwards. For it is true that late learners cannot so well take the ply; except it be in some minds that have not suffered themselves to fix, but have kept themselves open and prepared to receive continual amendment; which is exceeding rare. But if the force of custom simply and separate be great, the force of custom copulate and conjoined and collegiate is far greater. For there example teacheth, company comforteth, emulation quickeneth, glory raiseth; so as in such places the force of custom is in his exaltation. Certainly, the great multiplication of virtues upon human nature resteth upon societies well ordained and disciplined. For commonwealths and good governments do nourish virtue grown, but do not much mend the seeds. But the misery is, that the most effectual means are now applied to the ends least to be desired.

Essay XL.—OF FORTUNE

It cannot be denied but outward accidents conduce
much to fortune: favour, opportunity, death of others,
occasion fitting virtue. But chiefly the mould of a man's
fortune is in his own hands. *Faber quisque fortunæ
suæ*, saith the poet. And the most frequent of external
causes is, that the folly of one man is the fortune of
another. For no man prospers so suddenly as by others'
errors. *Serpens nisi serpentem comederit non fit draco.*
Overt and apparent virtues bring forth praise; but there
be secret and hidden virtues that bring forth fortune;
certain deliveries of a man's self, which have no name.
The Spanish name, *desemboltura,* partly expresseth them:
when there be not stonds nor restiveness in a man's
nature, but that the wheels of his mind keep way with
the wheels of his fortune. For so Livy (after he had de-
scribed Cato Major in these words, *In illo viro tantum
robur corporis et animi fuit, ut quocunque loco natus esset,
fortunam sibi facturus videretur*) falleth upon that, that
he had *versatile ingenium.* Therefore if a man look
sharply and attentively, he shall see Fortune: for though
she be blind, yet she is not invisible. The way of fortune
is like the milken way in the sky; which is a meeting or
knot of a number of small stars, not seen asunder, but
giving light together. So are there a number of little
and scarce discerned virtues, or rather faculties and
customs, that make men fortunate. The Italians note
some of them, such as a man would little think. When
they speak of one that cannot do amiss, they will throw
in into his other conditions, that he hath *poco di matto.*
And certainly there be not two more fortunate properties,
than to have a little of the fool, and not too much of the
honest. Therefore extreme lovers of their country or
masters were never fortunate, neither can they be. For
when a man placeth his thoughts without himself, he

goeth not his own way. An hasty fortune maketh an enterpriser and remover (the French hath it better, *entreprenant,* or *remuant*), but the exercised fortune maketh the able man. Fortune is to be honoured and respected, and it be but for her daughters, Confidence and Reputation. For those two felicity breedeth; the first within a man's self, the latter in others towards him. All wise men, to decline the envy of their own virtues, use to ascribe them to Providence and Fortune; for so they may the better assume them; and besides, it is greatness in a man to be the care of the higher powers. So Cæsar said to the pilot in the tempest, *Cæsarem portas, et fortunam ejus.* So Sylla chose the name of *Felix* and not of *Magnus.* And it hath been noted, that those that ascribe openly too much to their own wisdom and policy, end infortunate. It is written that Timotheus the Athenian, after he had, in the account he gave to the state of his government, often interlaced this speech, *And in this Fortune had no part,* never prospered in any thing he undertook afterwards. Certainly, there be whose fortunes are like Homer's verses, that have a slide and easiness more than the verses of other poets: as Plutarch saith of Timoleon's fortune, in respect of that of Agesilaus or Epaminondas. And that this should be, no doubt it is much in a man's self.

which ebb or flow with merchandizing. The fourth, that it bringeth the treasure of a realm or state into a few hands. For the usurer being at certainties, and others at uncertainties, at the end of the game most of the money will be in the box; and ever a state flourisheth when wealth is more equally spread. The fifth, that it beats down the price of land: for the employment of money is chiefly either merchandizing or purchasing; and usury waylays both. The sixth, that it doth dull and damp all industries, improvements, and new inventions, wherein money would be stirring, if it were not for this slug. The last, that it is the canker and ruin of many men's estates; which in process of time breeds a public poverty.

On the other side, the commodities of usury are: first, that howsoever usury in some respect hindereth merchandizing, yet in some other it advanceth it; for it is certain that the greatest part of trade is driven by young merchants upon borrowing at interest; so as, if the usurer either call in or keep back his money, there will ensue presently a great stand of trade. The second is, that were it not for this easy borrowing upon interest, men's necessities would draw upon them a most sudden undoing, in that they would be forced to sell their means (be it lands or goods) far under foot; and so, whereas usury doth but gnaw upon them, bad markets would swallow them quite up. As for mortgaging or pawning, it will little mend the matter: for either men will not take pawns without use; or if they do, they will look precisely for the forfeiture. I remember a cruel moneyed man in the country, that would say: The devil take this usury, it keeps us from forfeitures of mortgages and bonds. The third and last is, that it is a vanity to conceive that there would be ordinary borrowing without profit; and it is impossible to conceive the number of inconveniences that will ensue, if borrowing be cramped. Therefore to speak of the abolishing of usury is idle. All states have ever had it, in one kind or rate or other. So as that opinion must be sent to Utopia.

Of Usury

To speak now of the reformation and reiglement of usury; how the discommodities of it may be best avoided, and the commodities retained. It appears, by the balance of commodities and discommodities of usury, two things are to be reconciled. The one, that the tooth of usury be grinded, that it bite not too much; the other, that there be left open a means to invite moneyed men to lend to the merchants, for the continuing and quickening of trade. This cannot be done, except you introduce two several sorts of usury, a less and a greater. For if you reduce usury to one low rate, it will ease the common borrower, but the merchant will be to seek for money. And it is to be noted, that the trade of merchandize, being the most lucrative, may bear usury at a good rate; other contracts not so.

To serve both intentions, the way would be briefly thus. That there be two rates of usury; the one free and general for all; the other under licence only, to certain persons and in certain places of merchandizing. First, therefore, let usury in general be reduced to five in the hundred; and let that rate be proclaimed to be free and current; and let the state shut itself out to take any penalty for the same. This will preserve borrowing from any general stop or dryness. This will ease infinite borrowers in the country. This will, in good part, raise the price of land, because land purchased at sixteen years' purchase will yield six in the hundred and somewhat more, whereas this rate of interest yields but five. This, by like reason, will encourage and edge industrious and profitable improvements; because many will rather venture in that kind than take five in the hundred, especially having been used to greater profit. Secondly, let there be certain persons licensed to lend to known merchants upon usury at a higher rate; and let it be with the cautions following. Let the rate be, even with the merchant himself, somewhat more easy than that he used formerly to pay; for by that means all borrowers shall have some ease by this reformation, be he merchant or whosoever. Let it be no bank or common stock, but every man be master of his own money: not that I

125

altogether mislike banks, but they will hardly be brooked, in regard of certain suspicions. Let the state be answered some small matter for the licence, and the rest left to the lender; for if the abatement be but small, it will no whit discourage the lender. For he, for example, that took before ten or nine in the hundred, will sooner descend to eight in the hundred, than give over his trade of usury, and go from certain gains to gains of hazard. Let these licensed lenders be in number indefinite, but restrained to certain principal cities and towns of merchandizing; for then they will be hardly able to colour other men's moneys in the country: so as the licence of nine will not suck away the current rate of five; for no man will lend his moneys far off, nor put them into unknown hands.

If it be objected that this doth, in a sort, authorize usury, which before was in some places but permissive; the answer is, that it is better to mitigate usury by declaration, than to suffer it to rage by connivance.

Essay XLII.—OF YOUTH AND AGE

A MAN that is young in years may be old in hours, if he have lost no time. But that happeneth rarely. Generally, youth is like the first cogitations, not so wise as the second. For there is a youth in thoughts as well as in ages. And yet the invention of young men is more lively than that of the old; and imaginations stream into their minds better, and, as it were, more divinely. Natures that have much heat, and great and violent desires and perturbations, are not ripe for action till they have passed the meridian of their years: as it was with Julius Cæsar, and Septimius Severus. Of the latter of whom it is said, *Juventutem egit erroribus, imo furoribus, plenam.* And yet he was the ablest emperor, almost, of all the list. But reposed natures may do well in youth. As it is seen in Augustus Cæsar, Cosmus, Duke of Florence, Gaston de Foix, and others. On the other side, heat and vivacity in age is an excellent composition for business. Young men are fitter to invent than to judge; fitter for execution than for counsel; and fitter for new projects than for settled business. For the experience of age, in things that fall within the compass of it, directeth them; but in new things, abuseth them. The errors of young men are the ruin of business; but the errors of aged men amount but to this, that more might have been done, or sooner. Young men, in the conduct and manage of actions, embrace more than they can hold; stir more than they can quiet; fly to the end, without consideration of the means and degrees; pursue some few principles which they have chanced upon absurdly; care not to innovate, which draws unknown inconveniences; use extreme remedies at first; and, that which doubleth all errors, will not acknowledge or retract them; like an unready horse, that will neither stop nor turn. Men of age object too much, consult too long, adventure too little, repent too soon, and seldom drive business home to the full period, but content themselves with a mediocrity of success. Certainly, it is good to compound employments of both; for that will be good for the present, because the virtues of either age may correct the defects of both; and good for succession, that young men may be learners, while men in age are actors; and, lastly, good for extern accidents, because authority followeth old men, and favour and popularity youth. But for the moral part, perhaps youth will have the pre-eminence, as age hath for the politic. A certain rabbin, upon the text, *Your young men shall see visions, and your old men shall dream dreams*, inferreth that young men are admitted nearer to God than old, because vision is a clearer revelation than a dream. And certainly, the more a man drinketh of the world, the more it intoxicateth; and age doth profit rather in the powers of understanding, than in the virtues of the will and affections. There be some have an over-early ripeness in their years, which fadeth betimes. These are, first, such as have brittle wits, the edge whereof is soon turned; such as was Hermogenes the rhetorician, whose books are exceeding subtile, who afterwards waxed stupid. A second sort is of those that have some natural dispositions which have better grace in youth than in age; such as is a fluent and luxuriant speech, which becomes youth well, but not age: so Tully saith of Hortensius, *Idem manebat, neque idem docebat*. The third is of such as take too high a strain at the first, and are magnanimous more than tract of years can uphold. As was Scipio Africanus, of whom Livy saith in effect, *Ultima primis cedebant.*

Essay XLIII.—OF BEAUTY

Virtue is like a rich stone, best plain set: and surely virtue is best in a body that is comely, though not of delicate features; and that hath rather dignity of presence, than beauty of aspect. Neither is it almost seen, that very beautiful persons are otherwise of great virtue; as if nature were rather busy not to err, than in labour to produce excellency. And therefore they prove accomplished, but not of great spirit; and study rather behaviour than virtue. But this holds not always; for Augustus Cæsar, Titus Vespasianus, Philip le Bel of France, Edward the Fourth of England, Alcibiades of Athens, Ismael the Sophy of Persia, were all high and great spirits, and yet the most beautiful men of their times. In beauty, that of favour is more than that of colour, and that of decent and gracious motion more than that of favour. That is the best part of beauty, which a picture cannot express; no, nor the first sight of the life. There is no excellent beauty that hath not some strangeness in the proportion. A man cannot tell whether Apelles or Albert Durer were the more trifler; whereof the one would make a personage by geometrical proportions, the other, by taking the best parts out of divers faces to make one excellent. Such personages, I think, would please nobody but the painter that made them. Not but I think a painter may make a better face than ever was; but he must do it by a kind of felicity (as a musician that maketh an excellent air in music), and not by rule. A man shall see faces, that, if you examine them part by part, you shall find never a good, and yet all together do well. If it be true that the principal part of beauty is in decent motion, certainly it is no marvel though persons in years seem many times more amiable; *pulchrorum autumnus pulcher :* for no youth can be comely but by pardon, and considering the youth as to make up the comeliness. Beauty is as summer fruits, which are easy to corrupt, and cannot last: and for the most part it makes a dissolute youth, and an age a little out of countenance: but yet certainly again, if it light well, it maketh virtues shine, and vices blush.

Essay XLIV.—OF DEFORMITY

DEFORMED persons are commonly even with nature: for as nature hath done ill by them, so do they by nature; being for the most part (as the Scripture saith) *void of natural affection;* and so they have their revenge of nature. Certainly, there is a consent between the body and the mind; and where nature erreth in the one, she ventureth in the other. *Ubi peccat in uno, periclitatur in altero.* But because there is in man an election touching the frame of his mind, and a necessity in the frame of his body, the stars of natural inclination are sometimes obscured by the sun of discipline and virtue. Therefore it is good to consider of deformity, not as a sign, which is more deceivable, but as a cause, which seldom faileth of the effect. Whosoever hath any thing fixed in his person that doth induce contempt, hath also a perpetual spur in himself to rescue and deliver himself from scorn. Therefore all deformed persons are extreme bold: first, as in their own defence, as being exposed to scorn; but in process of time, by a general habit. Also, it stirreth in them industry, and especially of this kind, to watch and observe the weakness of others, that they may have somewhat to repay. Again, in their superiors, it quencheth jealousy towards them, as persons that they think they may at pleasure despise; and it layeth their competitors and emulators asleep, as never believing they should be in possibility of advancement, till they see them in possession. So that upon the matter, in a great wit, deformity is an advantage to rising. Kings in ancient times (and at this present in some countries) were wont to put great trust in eunuchs; because they that are envious towards all are more obnoxious and officious towards one. But yet their trust towards them hath rather been as to good spials and good whisperers, than good magistrates and officers. And much like is the reason of deformed persons. Still the ground is, they will, if they be of spirit, seek to free themselves from scorn; which must be either by virtue or malice; and therefore let it not be marvelled if sometimes they prove excellent persons; as was Agesilaus, Zanger the son of Solyman, Æsop, Gasca President of Peru; and Socrates may go likewise amongst them, with others.

Essay XLV.—OF BUILDING

Houses are built to live in, and not to look on; therefore let use be preferred before uniformity, except where both may be had. Leave the goodly fabrics of houses, for beauty only, to the enchanted palaces of the poets; who build them with small cost. He that builds a fair house upon an ill seat, committeth himself to prison. Neither do I reckon it an ill seat only where the air is unwholesome, but likewise where the air is unequal; as you shall see many fine seats set upon a knap of ground, environed with higher hills round about it; whereby the heat of the sun is pent in, and the wind gathereth as in troughs; so as you shall have, and that suddenly, as great diversity of heat and cold as if you dwelt in several places. Neither is it ill air only that maketh an ill seat, but ill ways, ill markets, and, if you will consult with Momus, ill neighbours. I speak not of many more: want of water; want of wood, shade, and shelter; want of fruitfulness, and mixture of grounds of several natures; want of prospect; want of level grounds; want of places, at some near distance, for sports of hunting, hawking, and races; too near the sea, too remote; having the commodity of navigable rivers, or the discommodity of their overflowing; too far off from great cities, which may hinder business; or too near them, which lurcheth all provisions, and maketh every thing dear; where a man hath a great living laid together, and where he is scanted: all which as it is impossible perhaps to find together, so it is good to know them and think of them, that a man may take as many as he can; and if he have several dwellings, that he sort them so, that what he wanteth in the one he may find in the other. Lucullus answered Pompey well; who, when he saw his stately galleries and rooms so large and lightsome, in one of his houses, said: *Surely an excellent place for summer, but how do you in winter ?* Lucullus answered: *Why, do you not think me as wise as some fowl are, that ever change their abode towards the winter ?*

To pass from the seat to the house itself; we will do as Cicero doth in the orator's art, who writes books *De Oratore,* and a book he entitles *Orator;* whereof the former delivers the precepts of the art, and the latter the perfection. We will therefore describe a princely palace, making a brief model thereof. For it is strange to see, now in Europe, such huge buildings as the Vatican and Escurial and some others be, and yet scarce a very fair room in them.

First, therefore, I say, you cannot have a perfect palace, except you have two several sides; a side for the banquet, as is spoken of in the book of *Hester,* and a side for the household; the one for feasts and triumphs, and the other for dwelling. I understand both these sides to be not only returns, but parts of the front; and to be uniform without, though severally partitioned within; and to be on both sides of a great and stately tower in the midst of the front, that, as it were, joineth them together on either hand. I would have on the side of the banquet, in front, one only goodly room above stairs, of some forty foot high; and under it, a room for a dressing or preparing place at times of triumphs. On the other side, which is the household side, I wish it divided at the first into a hall and a chapel (with a partition between), both of good state and bigness; and those not to go all the length, but to have at the further end a winter and a summer parlour, both fair. And under these rooms, a fair and large cellar, sunk under ground; and likewise some privy kitchens, with butteries and pantries, and the like. As for the tower, I would have it two stories, of eighteen foot high a-piece, above the two wings; and a goodly leads upon the top, railed with statuas interposed; and the same tower to be divided into rooms, as shall be thought fit. The stairs likewise to the upper rooms, let them be upon a fair open newel, and finely railed in with images of wood cast into a brass colour; and a

Of Building

very fair landing place at the top. But this to be, if you do not point any of the lower rooms for a dining place of servants. For otherwise you shall have the servants' dinner after your own: for the steam of it will come up as in a tunnel. And so much for the front. Only, I understand the height of the first stairs to be sixteen foot, which is the height of the lower room.

Beyond this front is there to be a fair court, but three sides of it of a far lower building than the front. And in all the four corners of that court, fair stair-cases, cast into turrets on the outside, and not within the row of buildings themselves. But those towers are not to be of the height of the front, but rather proportionable to the lower building. Let the court not be paved, for that striketh up a great heat in summer, and much cold in winter. But only some side alleys, with a cross, and the quarters to graze, being kept shorn, but not too near shorn. The row of return, on the banquet side, let it be all stately galleries; in which galleries let there be three, or five, fine cupolas in the length of it, placed at equal distance; and fine coloured windows of several works. On the household side, chambers of presence and ordinary entertainments, with some bed-chambers; and let all three sides be a double house, without thorough lights on the sides, that you may have rooms from the sun, both for forenoon and afternoon. Cast it also that you may have rooms both for summer and winter; shady for summer, and warm for winter. You shall have sometimes fair houses so full of glass, that one cannot tell where to become to be out of the sun or cold. For inbowed windows, I hold them of good use; (in cities, indeed, upright do better, in respect of the uniformity towards the street); for they be pretty retiring places for conference; and besides, they keep both the wind and sun off; for that which would strike almost thorough the room, doth scarce pass the window. But let them be but few, four in the court, on the sides only.

Beyond this court, let there be an inward court, of the same square and height; which is to be environed with

Essay XLVI.—OF GARDENS

God Almighty first planted a garden. And indeed it is the purest of human pleasures. It is the greatest refreshment to the spirits of man; without which, buildings and palaces are but gross handyworks: and a man shall ever see that when ages grow to civility and elegancy, men come to build stately sooner than to garden finely; as if gardening were the greater perfection. I do hold it, in the royal ordering of gardens, there ought to be gardens for all the months in the year; in which, severally, things of beauty may be then in season. For December and January and the latter part of November, you must take such things as are green all winter: holly; ivy; bays; juniper; cypress-trees; yew; pine-apple-trees; fir-trees; rosemary; lavender; periwinkle, the white, the purple, and the blue; germander; flags; orange-trees, lemon-trees, and myrtles, if they be stoved; and sweet marjoram, warm set. There followeth, for the latter part of January and February, the mezereon-tree, which then blossoms; crocus vernus, both the yellow and the gray; primroses; anemones; the early tulippa; hyacinthus orientalis; chamaïris; fritillaria. For March, there come violets, specially the single blue, which are the earliest; the yellow daffadil; the daisy; the almond-tree in blossom; the peach-tree in blossom; the cornelian-tree in blossom; sweet briar. In April follow, the double white violet; the wall-flower; the stock-gillyflower; the cowslip; flower-delices, and lilies of all natures; rosemary flowers; the tulippa; the double piony; the pale daffadil; the French honeysuckle; the cherry-tree in blossom; the dammasin and plum-trees in blossom; the white-thorn in leaf; the lilac-tree. In May and June come pinks of all sorts, specially the blush pink; roses of all kinds, except the musk, which comes later; honeysuckles; strawberries; bugloss;

columbine; the French marygold; flos Africanus; cherry-
tree in fruit; ribes; figs in fruit; rasps; vine flowers;
lavender in flowers; the sweet satyrian, with the white
flower; herba muscaria; lilium convallium; the apple-
tree in blossom. In July come gillyflowers of all varie-
ties; musk-roses; the lime-tree in blossom; early pears
and plums in fruit; ginnitings; quadlins. In August
come plums of all sorts in fruit; pears; apricocks; berberries; filberds; musk-melons; monks-hoods, of all
colours. In September come grapes; apples; poppies
of all colours; peaches; melocotones; nectarines; cornelians; wardens; quinces. In October and the
beginning of November come services; medlars; bullises; roses cut or removed to come late; hollyokes;
and such like. These particulars are for the climate of
London; but my meaning is perceived, that you may
have *ver perpetuum*, as the place affords.

And because the breath of flowers is far sweeter in
the air (where it comes and goes, like the warbling of
music) than in the hand, therefore nothing is more fit
for that delight, than to know what be the flowers and
plants that do best perfume the air. Roses, damask
and red, are fast flowers of their smells; so that you
may walk by a whole row of them, and find nothing of
their sweetness; yea, though it be in a morning's dew.
Bays likewise yield no smell as they grow. Rosemary
little; nor sweet marjoram. That which above all
others yields the sweetest smell in the air, is the violet;
specially the white double violet, which comes twice a
year; about the middle of April, and about Bartholo-
mewtide. Next to that is the musk-rose. Then the
strawberry-leaves dying, which [yield] a most excellent
cordial smell. Then the flower of the vines; it is a little
dust, like the dust of a bent, which grows upon the
cluster in the first coming forth. Then sweet-briar.
Then wall-flowers, which are very delightful to be set
under a parlour or lower chamber window. Then pinks
and gillyflowers, specially the matted pink and clove gillyflower. Then the flowers of the lime-tree. Then the
honeysuckles, so they be somewhat afar off. Of bean

flowers I speak not, because they are field flowers. But those which perfume the air most delightfully, not passed by as the rest, but being trodden upon and crushed, are three: that is, burnet, wild thyme, and water-mints. Therefore you are to set whole alleys of them, to have the pleasure when you walk or tread.

For gardens (speaking of those which are indeed prince-like, as we have done of buildings), the contents ought not well to be under thirty acres of ground, and to be divided into three parts: a green in the entrance; a heath or desert in the going forth; and the main garden in the midst; besides alleys on both sides. And I like well that four acres of ground be assigned to the green; six to the heath; four and four to either side; and twelve to the main garden. The green hath two pleasures: the one, because nothing is more pleasant to the eye than green grass kept finely shorn; the other, because it will give you a fair alley in the midst, by which you may go in front upon a stately hedge, which is to enclose the garden. But because the alley will be long, and, in great heat of the year or day, you ought not to buy the shade in the garden by going in the sun thorough the green, therefore you are, of either side the green, to plant a covert alley, upon carpenter's work, about twelve foot in height, by which you may go in shade into the garden. As for the making of knots or figures with divers-coloured earths, that they may lie under the windows of the house on that side which the garden stands, they be but toys: you may see as good sights many times in tarts. The garden is best to be square; encompassed, on all the four sides, with a stately arched hedge. The arches to be upon pillars of carpenter's work, of some ten foot high and six foot broad; and the spaces between of the same dimension with the breadth of the arch. Over the arches let there be an entire hedge, of some four foot high, framed also upon carpenter's work; and upon the upper hedge, over every arch, a little turret, with a belly, enough to receive a cage of birds; and over every space between the arches some other little figure, with broad plates of round coloured glass, gilt, for the sun to play upon. But this hedge I intend to be raised upon a bank, not steep, but gently slope, of some six foot, set all with flowers. Also I understand that this square of the garden should not be the whole breadth of the ground, but to leave, on either side, ground enough for diversity of side alleys; unto which the two covert alleys of the green may deliver you. But there must be no alleys with hedges at either end of this great enclosure: not at the hither end, for letting your prospect upon this fair hedge from the green; nor at the further end, for letting your prospect from the hedge, through the arches, upon the heath.

For the ordering of the ground within the great hedge, I leave it to variety of device; advising, nevertheless, that whatsoever form you cast it into, first, it be not too busy or full of work. Wherein I, for my part, do not like images cut out in juniper or other garden stuff: they be for children. Little low hedges, round, like welts, with some pretty pyramides, I like well; and in some places, fair columns upon frames of carpenter's work. I would also have the alleys spacious and fair. You may have closer alleys upon the side grounds, but none in the main garden. I wish also, in the very middle, a fair mount, with three ascents, and alleys, enough for four to walk abreast; which I would have to be perfect circles, without any bulwarks or embossments; and the whole mount to be thirty foot high; and some fine banqueting-house, with some chimneys neatly cast, and without too much glass.

For fountains, they are a great beauty and refreshment; but pools mar all, and make the garden unwholesome and full of flies and frogs. Fountains I intend to be of two natures: the one, that sprinkleth or spouteth water; the other, a fair receipt of water, of some thirty or forty foot square, but without fish, or slime, or mud. For the first, the ornaments of images gilt, or of marble, which are in use, do well: but the main matter is, so to convey the water, as it never stay, either in the bowls or in the cistern; that the water be never by rest discoloured, green or red or the like, or gather any mossiness or putrefaction. Besides that, it is to be cleansed every day by the hand. Also some steps up to it, and some fine pavement about it, doth well. As for the other kind of fountain, which we may call a bathing pool, it may admit much curiosity and beauty, wherewith we will not trouble ourselves: as, that the bottom be finely paved, and with images; the sides likewise; and withal embellished with coloured glass, and such things of lustre; encompassed also with fine rails of low statuas. But the main point is the same which we mentioned in the former kind of fountain; which is, that the water be in perpetual motion, fed by a water higher than the pool, and delivered into it by fair spouts, and then discharged away under ground, by some equality of bores, that it stay little. And for fine devices, of arching water without spilling, and making it rise in several forms (of feathers, drinking glasses, canopies, and the like), they be pretty things to look on, but nothing to health and sweetness.

For the heath, which was the third part of our plot, I wish it to be framed, as much as may be, to a natural wildness. Trees I would have none in it; but some thickets, made only of sweet-briar and honeysuckle, and some wild vine amongst; and the ground set with violets, strawberries, and primroses. For these are sweet, and prosper in the shade. And these to be in the heath, here and there, not in any order. I like also little heaps, in the nature of mole-hills (such as are in wild heaths), to be set, some with wild thyme; some with pinks; some with germander, that gives a good flower to the eye; some with periwinkle; some with violets; some with strawberries; some with cowslips; some with daisies; some with red roses; some with lilium convallium; some with sweet-williams red; some with bear's-foot; and the like low flowers, being withal sweet and sightly. Part of which heaps to be with standards of little bushes pricked upon their top, and part without. The standards to be roses; juniper;

holly; berberries (but here and there, because of the smell of their blossom); red currans; gooseberries; rosemary; bays; sweet-briar; and such like. But these standards to be kept with cutting, that they grow not out of course.

For the side grounds, you are to fill them with variety of alleys, private, to give a full shade, some of them, wheresoever the sun be. You are to frame some of them likewise for shelter, that when the wind blows sharp, you may walk as in a gallery. And those alleys must be likewise hedged at both ends, to keep out the wind; and these closer alleys must be ever finely gravelled, and no grass, because of going wet. In many of these alleys likewise, you are to set fruit-trees of all sorts; as well upon the walls as in ranges. And this would be generally observed, that the borders, wherein you plant your fruit-trees, be fair and large, and low, and not steep; and set with fine flowers, but thin and sparingly, lest they deceive the trees. At the end of both the side grounds, I would have a mount of some pretty height, leaving the wall of the enclosure breast high, to look abroad into the fields.

For the main garden, I do not deny but there should be some fair alleys, ranged on both sides with fruit-trees; and some pretty tufts of fruit-trees, and arbours with seats, set in some decent order; but these to be by no means set too thick; but to leave the main garden so as it be not close, but the air open and free. For as for shade, I would have you rest upon the alleys of the side grounds, there to walk, if you be disposed, in the heat of the year or day; but to make account that the main garden is for the more temperate parts of the year; and in the heat of summer, for the morning and the evening, or over-cast days.

For aviaries, I like them not, except they be of that largeness as they may be turfed, and have living plants and bushes set in them; that the birds may have more scope and natural nestling, and that no foulness appear in the floor of the aviary. So I have made a platform of a princely garden, partly by precept, partly by draw-

Of Gardens

ing, not a model, but some general lines of it; and in this I have spared for no cost. But it is nothing for great princes, that, for the most part, taking advice with workmen, with no less cost set their things together; and sometimes add statuas, and such things, for state and magnificence, but nothing to the true pleasure of a garden.

Essay XLVII.—OF NEGOCIATING

It is generally better to deal by speech than by letter; and by the mediation of a third than by a man's self. Letters are good, when a man would draw an answer by letter back again; or when it may serve for a man's justification afterwards to produce his own letter; or where it may be danger to be interrupted, or heard by pieces. To deal in person is good, when a man's face breedeth regard, as commonly with inferiors; or in tender cases, where a man's eye upon the countenance of him with whom he speaketh may give him a direction how far to go; and generally, where a man will reserve to himself liberty either to disavow or to expound. In choice of instruments, it is better to choose men of a plainer sort, that are like to do that that is committed to them, and to report back again faithfully the success, than those that are cunning to contrive out of other men's business somewhat to grace themselves, and will help the matter in report for satisfaction sake. Use also such persons as effect the business wherein they are employed; for that quickeneth much; and such as are fit for the matter; as bold men for expostulation, fair-spoken men for persuasion, crafty men for inquiry and observation, froward and absurd men for business that doth not well bear out itself. Use also such as have been lucky and prevailed before in things wherein you have employed them; for that breeds confidence, and they will strive to maintain their prescription. It is better to sound a person, with whom one deals, afar off, than to fall upon the point at first; except you mean to surprise him by some short question. It is better dealing with men in appetite, than with those that are where they would be. If a man deal with another upon conditions, the start or first performance is all; which a man cannot reasonably demand, except

Of Negociating

either the nature of the thing be such which must go before; or else a man can persuade the other party that he shall still need him in some other thing; or else that he be counted the honester man. All practice is to discover, or to work. Men discover themselves in trust; in passion; at unawares; and of necessity, when they would have somewhat done and cannot find an apt pretext. If you would work any man, you must either know his nature and fashions, and so lead him; or his ends, and so persuade him; or his weakness and disadvantages, and so awe him; or those that have interest in him, and so govern him. In dealing with cunning persons, we must ever consider their ends, to interpret their speeches; and it is good to say little to them, and that which they least look for. In all negociations of difficulty, a man may not look to sow and reap at once; but must prepare business, and so ripen it by degrees.

Essay XLVIII.—OF FOLLOWERS AND FRIENDS

Costly followers are not to be liked; lest while a man maketh his train longer, he make his wings shorter. I reckon to be costly, not them alone which charge the purse, but which are wearisome and importune in suits. Ordinary followers ought to challenge no higher conditions than countenance, recommendation, and protection from wrongs. Factious followers are worse to be liked, which follow not upon affection to him with whom they range themselves, but upon discontentment conceived against some other: whereupon commonly ensueth that ill intelligence that we many times see between great personages. Likewise glorious followers, who make themselves as trumpets of the commendation of those they follow, are full of inconvenience; for they taint business through want of secrecy; and they export honour from a man, and make him a return in envy. There is a kind of followers likewise which are dangerous, being indeed espials; which inquire the secrets of the house, and bear tales of them to others. Yet such men, many times, are in great favour; for they are officious, and commonly exchange tales. The following by certain estates of men, answerable to that which a great person himself professeth (as of soldiers to him that hath been employed in the wars, and the like), hath ever been a thing civil, and well taken even in monarchies; so it be without too much pomp or popularity. But the most honourable kind of following is to be followed as one that apprehendeth to advance virtue and desert in all sorts of persons. And yet, where there is no eminent odds in sufficiency, it is better to take with the more passable than with the more able. And besides, to speak truth, in base times active men are of more use than virtuous.

Of Followers and Friends

It is true that, in government, it is good to use men of one rank equally: for to countenance some extraordinarily is to make them insolent, and the rest discontent; because they may claim a due. But contrariwise, in favour, to use men with much difference and election is good; for it maketh the persons preferred more thankful, and the rest more officious; because all is of favour. It is good discretion not to make too much of any man at the first; because one cannot hold out that proportion. To be governed (as we call it) by one is not safe; for it shews softness, and gives a freedom to scandal and disreputation; for those that would not censure or speak ill of a man immediately, will talk more boldly of those that are so great with them, and thereby wound their honour. Yet to be distracted with many is worse; for it makes men to be of the last impression, and full of change. To take advice of some few friends is ever honourable; *for lookers-on many times see more than gamesters; and the vale best discovereth the hill.* There is little friendship in the world, and least of all between equals, which was wont to be magnified. That that is, is between superior and inferior, whose fortunes may comprehend the one the other.

Essay XLIX.—OF SUITORS

MANY ill matters and projects are undertaken; and private suits do putrefy the public good. Many good matters are undertaken with bad minds; I mean not only corrupt minds, but crafty minds, that intend not performance. Some embrace suits, which never mean to deal effectually in them; but if they see there may be life in the matter by some other mean, they will be content to win a thank, or take a second reward, or at least to make use, in the mean time, of the suitor's hopes. Some take hold of suits only for an occasion to cross some other: or to make an information, whereof they could not otherwise have apt pretext; without care what become of the suit when that turn is served; or, generally, to make other men's business a kind of entertainment to bring in their own. Nay, some undertake suits with a full purpose to let them fall, to the end to gratify the adverse party or competitor. Surely there is in some sort a right in every suit: either a right of equity, if it be a suit of controversy; or a right of desert, if it be a suit of petition. If affection lead a man to favour the wrong side in justice, let him rather use his countenance to compound the matter than to carry it. If affection lead a man to favour the less worthy in desert, let him do it without depraving or disabling the better deserver. In suits which a man doth not well understand, it is good to refer them to some friend of trust and judgement, that may report whether he may deal in them with honour: but let him choose well his referendaries, for else he may be led by the nose. Suitors are so distasted with delays and abuses, that plain dealing, in denying to deal in suits at first, and reporting the success barely, and in challenging no more thanks than one hath deserved, is grown not only honourable but also gracious. In suits of favour, the

Of Suitors

first coming ought to take little place: so far forth consideration may be had of his trust, that if intelligence of the matter could not otherwise have been had but by him, advantage be not taken of the note, but the party left to his other means, and in some sort recompensed for his discovery. To be ignorant of the value of a suit is simplicity; as well as to be ignorant of the right thereof is want of conscience. Secrecy in suits is a great mean of obtaining; for voicing them to be in forwardness may discourage some kind of suitors, but doth quicken and awake others. But timing of the suit is the principal. Timing, I say, not only in respect of the person that should grant it, but in respect of those which are like to cross it. Let a man, in the choice of his mean, rather choose the fittest mean than the greatest mean; and rather them that deal in certain things than those that are general. The reparation of a denial is sometimes equal to the first grant, if a man shew himself neither dejected nor discontented. *Iniquum petas, ut æquum feras*, is a good rule, where a man hath strength of favour: but otherwise, a man were better rise in his suit; for he that would have ventured at first to have lost the suitor, will not in the conclusion lose both the suitor and his own former favour. Nothing is thought so easy a request to a great person as his letter; and yet, if it be not in a good cause, it is so much out of his reputation. There are no worse instruments than these general contrivers of suits; for they are but a kind of poison and infection to public proceedings.

Essay L.—OF STUDIES

STUDIES serve for delight, for ornament, and for ability. Their chief use for delight is in privateness and retiring; for ornament, is in discourse; and for ability, is in the judgement and disposition of business. For expert men can execute, and perhaps judge of particulars, one by one; but the general counsels, and the plots and marshalling of affairs, come best from those that are learned. To spend too much time in studies is sloth; to use them too much for ornament is affectation; to make judgement wholly by their rules is the humour of a scholar. They perfect nature, and are perfected by experience; for natural abilities are like natural plants, that need proyning by study; and studies themselves do give forth directions too much at large, except they be bounded in by experience. Crafty men contemn studies; simple men admire them; and wise men use them: for they teach not their own use; but that is a wisdom without them and above them, won by observation. Read not to contradict and confute; nor to believe and take for granted; nor to find talk and discourse; but to weigh and consider. Some books are to be tasted, others to be swallowed, and some few to be chewed and digested: that is, some books are to be read only in parts; others to be read, but not curiously; and some few to be read wholly, and with diligence and attention. Some books also may be read by deputy, and extracts made of them by others; but that would be only in the less important arguments, and the meaner sort of books; else distilled books are like common distilled waters, flashy things. Reading maketh a full man; conference a ready man; and writing an exact man. And therefore, if a man write little, he had need have a great memory; if he confer little, he had need have

Of Studies

a present wit; and if he read little, he had need have much cunning, to seem to know that he doth not. Histories make men wise; poets witty; the mathematics subtile; natural philosophy deep; moral grave; logic and rhetoric able to contend. *Abeunt studia in mores.* Nay, there is no stond or impediment in the wit, but may be wrought out by fit studies: like as diseases of the body may have appropriate exercises. Bowling is good for the stone and reins; shooting for the lungs and breast; gentle walking for the stomach; riding for the head; and the like. So if a man's wit be wandering, let him study the mathematics; for in demonstrations, if his wit be called away never so little, he must begin again: if his wit be not apt to distinguish or find differences, let him study the schoolmen; for they are *cymini sectores :* if he be not apt to beat over matters, and to call one thing to prove and illustrate another, let him study the lawyers' cases: so every defect of the mind may have a special receipt.

Essay LI.—OF FACTION

MANY have an opinion not wise, that for a prince to govern his estate, or for a great person to govern his proceedings, according to the respect of factions, is a principal part of policy: whereas contrariwise, the chiefest wisdom is either in ordering those things which are general, and wherein men of several factions do nevertheless agree; or in dealing with correspondence to particular persons, one by one. But I say not that the consideration of factions is to be neglected. Mean men, in their rising, must adhere; but great men, that have strength in themselves, were better to maintain themselves indifferent and neutral. Yet even in beginners, to adhere so moderately, as he be a man of the one faction which is most passable with the other, commonly giveth best way. The lower and weaker faction is the firmer in conjunction; and it is often seen that a few that are stiff do tire out a greater number that are more moderate. When one of the factions is extinguished, the remaining subdivideth: as the faction between Lucullus and the rest of the nobles of the senate (which they called *Optimates*) held out a while against the faction of Pompey and Cæsar; but when the senate's authority was pulled down, Cæsar and Pompey soon after brake. The faction or party of Antonius and Octavianus Cæsar, against Brutus and Cassius, held out likewise for a time; but when Brutus and Cassius were overthrown, then soon after Antonius and Octavianus brake and subdivided. These examples are of wars, but the same holdeth in private factions. And therefore those that are seconds in factions do many times, when the faction subdivideth, prove principals: but many times also they prove cyphers and cashiered; for many a man's strength is in opposition, and when that faileth,

Of Faction

he groweth out of use. It is commonly seen that men once placed take in with the contrary faction to that by which they enter; thinking belike that they have the first sure, and now are ready for a new purchase. The traitor in faction lightly goeth away with it; for when matters have stuck long in balancing, the winning of some one man casteth them, and he getteth all the thanks. The even carriage between two factions proceedeth not always of moderation, but of a trueness to a man's self, with end to make use of both. Certainly in Italy they hold it a little suspect in popes, when they have often in their mouth *Padre commune;* and take it to be a sign of one that meaneth to refer all to the greatness of his own house. Kings had need beware how they side themselves, and make themselves as of a faction or party; for leagues within the state are ever pernicious to monarchies; for they raise an obligation paramount to obligation of sovereignty, and make the king *tanquam unus ex nobis:* as was to be seen in the League of France. When factions are carried too high and too violently, it is a sign of weakness in princes, and much to the prejudice both of their authority and business. The motions of factions under kings ought to be like the motions (as the astronomers speak) of the inferior orbs; which may have their proper motions, but yet still are quietly carried by the higher motion of *primum mobile.*

Essay LII.—OF CEREMONIES AND RESPECTS

HE that is only real had need have exceeding great parts of virtue; as the stone had need to be rich that is set without foil. But if a man mark it well, it is in praise and commendation of men as it is in gettings and gains: for the proverb is true, *that light gains make heavy purses;* for light gains come thick, whereas great come but now and then. So it is true that small matters win great commendation, because they are continually in use and in note: whereas the occasion of any great virtue cometh but on festivals. Therefore it doth much add to a man's reputation, and is (as Queen Isabella said) *like perpetual letters commendatory,* to have good forms. To attain them, it almost sufficeth not to despise them; for so shall a man observe them in others; and let him trust himself with the rest. For if he labour too much to express them, he shall lose their grace; which is to be natural and unaffected. Some men's behaviour is like a verse, wherein every syllable is measured: how can a man comprehend great matters, that breaketh his mind too much to small observations? Not to use ceremonies at all is to teach others not to use them again, and so diminisheth respect to himself; especially they be not to be omitted to strangers and formal natures; but the dwelling upon them, and exalting them above the moon, is not only tedious, but doth diminish the faith and credit of him that speaks. And certainly there is a kind of conveying of effectual and imprinting passages amongst compliments, which is of singular use, if a man can hit upon it. Amongst a man's peers, a man shall be sure of familiarity; and therefore it is good a little to keep state. Amongst a man's inferiors, one shall be sure of reverence; and therefore it is good a

Of Ceremonies and Respects

little to be familiar. He that is too much in any thing, so that he giveth another occasion of satiety, maketh himself cheap. To apply one's self to others is good; so it be with demonstration that a man doth it upon regard, and not upon facility. It is a good precept generally in seconding another, yet to add somewhat of one's own: as, if you will grant his opinion, let it be with some distinction; if you will follow his motion, let it be with condition; if you will allow his counsel, let it be with alleging further reason. Men had need beware how they be too perfect in compliments; for be they never so sufficient otherwise, their enviers will be sure to give them that attribute, to the disadvantage of their greater virtues. It is loss also in business to be too full of respects, or to be too curious in observing times and opportunities. Salomon saith, *He that considereth the wind shall not sow, and he that looketh to the clouds shall not reap.* A wise man will make more opportunities than he finds. Men's behaviour should be like their apparel, not too strait or point device, but free for exercise or motion.

Essay LIII.—OF PRAISE

PRAISE is the reflection of virtue. But it is as the glass or body which giveth the reflection. If it be from the common people, it is commonly false and naught; and rather followeth vain persons than virtuous. For the common people understand not many excellent virtues. The lowest virtues draw praise from them; the middle virtues work in them astonishment or admiration; but of the highest virtues they have no sense or perceiving at all. But shews, and *species virtutibus similes*, serve best with them. Certainly, fame is like a river, that beareth up things light and swoln, and drowns things weighty and solid. But if persons of quality and judgement concur, then it is as the Scripture saith, *Nomen bonum instar unguenti fragrantis:* it filleth all round about, and will not easily away: for the odours of ointments are more durable than those of flowers. There be so many false points of praise, that a man may justly hold it a suspect. Some praises proceed merely of flattery: and if he be an ordinary flatterer, he will have certain common attributes, which may serve every man: if he be a cunning flatterer, he will follow the arch-flatterer, which is a man's self; and wherein a man thinketh best of himself, therein the flatterer will uphold him most: but if he be an impudent flatterer, look wherein a man is conscious to himself that he is most defective and is most out of countenance in himself, that will the flatterer entitle him to perforce, *spretâ conscientiâ.* Some praises come of good wishes and respects, which is a form due in civility to kings and great persons, *laudando præcipere;* when by telling men what they are, they represent to them what they should be. Some men are praised maliciously to their hurt, thereby to stir envy and jealousy towards them; *pessimum genus inimicorum*

156

Of Praise

laudantium; insomuch as it was a proverb amongst the Grecians, that *he that was praised to his hurt should have a push rise upon his nose :* as we say, *that a blister will rise upon one's tongue that tells a lie.* Certainly moderate praise, used with opportunity, and not vulgar, is that which doth the good. Salomon saith, *He that praiseth his friend aloud, rising early, it shall be to him no better than a curse.* Too much magnifying of man or matter doth irritate contradiction, and procure envy and scorn. To praise a man's self cannot be decent, except it be in rare cases; but to praise a man's office or profession, he may do it with good grace, and with a kind of magnanimity. The cardinals of Rome, which are theologues, and friars, and schoolmen, have a phrase of notable contempt and scorn towards civil business: for they call all temporal business, of wars, embassages, judicature, and other employments, *sbirrerie,* which is *under-sheriffries,* as if they were but matters for under-sheriffs and catchpoles; though many times those *under-sheriffries* do more good than their high speculations. St. Paul, when he boasts of himself, he doth oft interlace, *I speak like a fool ;* but speaking of his calling, he saith, *Magnificabo apostolatum meum.*

Essay LIV.—OF VAIN-GLORY

It was prettily devised of Æsop: *The fly sate upon the axle-tree of the chariot wheel, and said, What a dust do I raise!* So are there some vain persons, that, whatsoever goeth alone or moveth upon greater means, if they have never so little hand in it, they think it is they that carry it. They that are glorious must needs be factious; for all bravery stands upon comparisons. They must needs be violent, to make good their own vaunts. Neither can they be secret, and therefore not effectual; but according to the French proverb, *beaucoup de bruit, peu de fruit; much bruit, little fruit.* Yet certainly there is use of this quality in civil affairs. Where there is an opinion and fame to be created, either of virtue or greatness, these men are good trumpeters. Again, as Titus Livius noteth, in the case of Antiochus and the Ætolians, *There are sometimes great effects of cross lies;* as, if a man that negotiates between two princes to draw them to join in a war against the third, doth extol the forces of either of them above measure, the one to the other: and sometimes he that deals between man and man raiseth his own credit with both, by pretending greater interest than he hath in either. And in these and the like kinds, it often falls out that somewhat is produced of nothing; for lies are sufficient to breed opinion, and opinion brings on substance. In militar commanders and soldiers, vain-glory is an essential point; for as iron sharpens iron, so by glory one courage sharpeneth another. In cases of great enterprise, upon charge and adventure, a composition of glorious natures doth put life into business; and those that are of solid and sober natures have more of the ballast than of the sail. In fame of learning, the flight will be slow without some feathers of ostentation. *Qui de contemnendâ gloriâ libros scribunt,*

Of Vain-Glory

nomen suum inscribunt. Socrates, Aristotle, Galen, were
men full of ostentation. Certainly vain-glory helpeth
to perpetuate a man's memory; and virtue was never so
beholding to human nature, as it received his due at
the second hand. Neither had the fame of Cicero,
Seneca, Plinius Secundus, borne her age so well, if it
had not been joined with some vanity in themselves:
like unto varnish, that makes seelings not only shine
but last. But all this while, when I speak of vain-glory,
I mean not of that property that Tacitus doth attribute
to Mucianus; *Omnium, quæ dixerat feceratque, arte
quâdam ostentator ;* for that proceeds not of vanity, but
of natural magnanimity and discretion; and in some
persons is not only comely, but gracious. For excusations, cessions, modesty itself well governed, are but
arts of ostentation. And amongst those arts there is
none better than that which Plinius Secundus speaketh
of, which is to be liberal of praise and commendation
to others, in that wherein a man's self hath any perfection. For saith Pliny very wittily: *In commending
another you do yourself right ; for he that you commend
is either superior to you in that you commend, or inferior.
If he be inferior, if he be to be commended, you much
more ; if he be superior, if he be not to be commended, you
much less.* Glorious men are the scorn of wise men;
the admiration of fools; the idols of parasites; and the
slaves of their own vaunts.

Essay LV.—OF HONOUR AND REPUTATION

THE winning of honour is but the revealing of a man's virtue and worth without disadvantage. For some in their actions do woo and affect honour and reputation; which sort of men are commonly much talked of, but inwardly little admired. And some, contrariwise, darken their virtue in the shew of it; so as they be undervalued in opinion. If a man perform that which hath not been attempted before; or attempted and given over; or hath been achieved, but not with so good circumstance; he shall purchase more honour, than by effecting a matter of greater difficulty or virtue, wherein he is but a follower. If a man so temper his actions, as in some one of them he doth content every faction or combination of people, the music will be the fuller. A man is an ill husband of his honour, that entreth into any action, the failing wherein may disgrace him more than the carrying of it through can honour him. Honour that is gained and broken upon another hath the quickest reflection; like diamonds cut with facets. And therefore let a man contend to excel any competitors of his in honour, in outshooting them, if he can, in their own bow. Discreet followers and servants help much to reputation: *Omnis fama a domesticis emanat.* Envy, which is the canker of honour, is best extinguished by declaring a man's self in his ends rather to seek merit than fame; and by attributing a man's successes rather to divine Providence and felicity, than to his own virtue or policy. The true marshalling of the degrees of sovereign honour are these. In the first place are *conditores imperiorum*, founders of states and commonwealths; such as were Romulus, Cyrus, Cæsar, Ottoman, Ismael. In the second place are *legis-latores*, law-givers; which are

Of Honour and Reputation

also called *second founders*, or *perpetui principes*, because they govern by their ordinances after they are gone: such were Lycurgus, Solon, Justinian, Eadgar, Alphonsus of Castile the Wise, that made the *Siete Partidas*. In the third place are *liberatores*, or *salvatores*; such as compound the long miseries of civil wars, or deliver their countries from servitude of strangers or tyrants; as Augustus Cæsar, Vespasianus, Aurelianus, Theodoricus, K. Henry the VII. of England, K. Henry the IV. of France. In the fourth place are *propagatores* or *propugnatores imperii*; such as in honourable wars enlarge their territories, or make noble defence against invaders. And in the last place are *patres patriæ*, which reign justly, and make the times good wherein they live. Both which last kinds need no examples, they are in such number. Degrees of honour in subjects are: first, *participes curarum*; those upon whom princes do discharge the greatest weight of their affairs; their *right hands*, as we call them. The next are *duces belli*, great leaders; such as are princes' lieutenants and do them notable services in the wars. The third are *gratiosi*, favourites; such as exceed not this scantling, to be solace to the sovereign and harmless to the people. And the fourth, *negotiis pares*; such as have great places under princes, and execute their places with sufficiency. There is an honour, likewise, which may be ranked amongst the greatest, which happeneth rarely; that is, of such as sacrifice themselves to death or danger for the good of their country; as was M. Regulus, and the two Decii.

Essay LVI.—OF JUDICATURE

Judges ought to remember that their office is *jus dicere*, and not *jus dare*; to interpret law, and not to make law, or give law. Else will it be like the authority claimed by the church of Rome; which, under pretext of exposition of Scripture, doth not stick to add and alter, and to pronounce that which they do not find, and by shew of antiquity to introduce novelty. Judges ought to be more learned than witty, more reverend than plausible, and more advised than confident. Above all things, integrity is their portion and proper virtue. *Cursed* (saith the law) *is he that removeth the land-mark*. The mislayer of a meere stone is to blame. But it is the unjust judge that is the capital remover of land-marks, when he defineth amiss of lands and property. One foul sentence doth more hurt than many foul examples. For these do but corrupt the stream; the other corrupteth the fountain. So saith Salomon: *Fons turbatus, et vena corrupta, est justus cadens in causâ suâ coram adversario.* The office of judges may have reference unto the parties that sue; unto the advocates that plead; unto the clerks and ministers of justice underneath them; and to the sovereign or state above them.

First, for the causes or parties that sue. *There be* (saith the Scripture) *that turn judgement into wormwood;* and surely there be also that turn it into vinegar; for injustice maketh it bitter, and delays make it sour. The principal duty of a judge is to suppress force and fraud; whereof force is the more pernicious when it is open, and fraud when it is close and disguised. Add thereto contentious suits, which ought to be spewed out, as the surfeit of courts. A judge ought to prepare his way to a just sentence, as God useth to prepare his way, by *raising valleys* and *taking down hills*: so when

boldness of advocates should prevail with judges; whereas they should imitate God, in whose seat they sit; who *represseth the presumptuous*, and *giveth grace to the modest*. But it is more strange, that judges should have noted favourites; which cannot but cause multiplication of fees, and suspicion of by-ways. There is due from the judge to the advocate some commendation and gracing, where causes are well handled and fair pleaded; especially towards the side which obtaineth not; for that upholds in the client the reputation of his counsel, and beats down in him the conceit of his cause. There is likewise due to the public a civil reprehension of advocates, where there appeareth cunning counsel, gross neglect, slight information, indiscreet pressing, or an over-bold defence. And let not the counsel at the bar chop with the judge, nor wind himself into the handling of the cause anew after the judge hath declared his sentence: but on the other side, let not the judge meet the cause half way, nor give occasion to the party to say, *his counsel or proofs were not heard*.

Thirdly, for that that concerns clerks and ministers. The place of justice is an hallowed place; and therefore not only the bench, but the foot-pace and precincts and purprise thereof, ought to be preserved without scandal and corruption. For certainly, *Grapes* (as the Scripture saith) *will not be gathered of thorns or thistles;* neither can justice yield her fruit with sweetness amongst the briars and brambles of catching and polling clerks and ministers. The attendance of courts is subject to four bad instruments. First, certain persons that are sowers of suits; which make the court swell, and the country pine. The second sort is of those that engage courts in quarrels of jurisdiction, and are not truly *amici curiæ*, but *parasiti curiæ*, in puffing a court up beyond her bounds, for their own scraps and advantage. The third sort is of those that may be accounted the left hands of courts; persons that are full of nimble and sinister tricks and shifts, whereby they pervert the plain and direct courses of courts, and bring justice into oblique lines and labyrinths. And the fourth is the

Of Judicature

poller and exacter of fees; which justifies the common resemblance of the courts of justice to the bush, whereunto while the sheep flies for defence in weather, he is sure to lose part of his fleece. On the other side, an ancient clerk, skilful in precedents, wary in proceeding, and understanding in the business of the court, is an excellent finger of a court, and doth many times point the way to the judge himself.

Fourthly, for that which may concern the sovereign and estate. Judges ought above all to remember the conclusion of the Roman Twelve Tables, *Salus populi suprema lex;* and to know that laws, except they be in order to that end, are but things captious, and oracles not well inspired. Therefore it is an happy thing in a state when kings and states do often consult with judges; and again, when judges do often consult with the king and state: the one, when there is matter of law intervenient in business of state; the other, when there is some consideration of state intervenient in matter of law. For many times the things deduced to judgement may be *meum* and *tuum*, when the reason and consequence thereof may trench to point of estate: I call matter of estate, not only the parts of sovereignty, but whatsoever introduceth any great alteration or dangerous precedent, or concerneth manifestly any great portion of people. And let no man weakly conceive that just laws and true policy have any antipathy: for they are like the spirits and sinews, that one moves with the other. Let judges also remember that Salomon's throne was supported by lions on both sides: let them be lions, but yet lions under the throne; being circumspect that they do not check or oppose any points of sovereignty. Let not judges also be so ignorant of their own right, as to think there is not left to them, as a principal part of their office, a wise use and application of laws. For they may remember what the Apostle saith of a greater law than theirs: *Nos scimus quia lex bona est, modo quis eâ utatur legitime.*

ESSAY LVII.—OF ANGER

To seek to extinguish anger utterly is but a bravery of
the Stoics. We have better oracles: *Be angry, but sin
not. Let not the sun go down upon your anger.* Anger
must be limited and confined, both in race and in time.
We will first speak, how the natural inclination and habit
to be angry may be attempered and calmed. Secondly,
how the particular motions of anger may be repressed,
or at least refrained from doing mischief. Thirdly, how
to raise anger, or appease anger, in another.

For the first; there is no other way but to meditate
and ruminate well upon the effects of anger, how it
troubles man's life. And the best time to do this is to
look back upon anger when the fit is throughly over.
Seneca saith well, *that anger is like ruin, which breaks itself upon that it falls.* The Scripture exhorteth us *to
possess our souls in patience.* Whosoever is out of
patience, is out of possession of his soul. Men must
not turn bees;

——animasque in vulnere ponunt.

Anger is certainly a kind of baseness; as it appears well
in the weakness of those subjects in whom it reigns;
children, women, old folks, sick folks. Only men must
beware that they carry their anger rather with scorn than
with fear; so that they may seem rather to be above the
injury than below it: which is a thing easily done, if a
man will give law to himself in it.

For the second point; the causes and motives of anger
are chiefly three. First, to be too sensible of hurt: for
no man is angry that feels not himself hurt: and therefore tender and delicate persons must needs be oft
angry; they have so many things to trouble them, which
more robust natures have little sense of. The next is,
the apprehension and construction of the injury offered

Of Anger

to be, in the circumstances thereof, full of contempt.
For contempt is that which putteth an edge upon anger,
as much or more than the hurt itself. And therefore,
when men are ingenious in picking out circumstances of
contempt, they do kindle their anger much. Lastly,
opinion of the touch of a man's reputation doth multiply
and sharpen anger. Wherein the remedy is, that a man
should have, as Consalvo was wont to say, *telam honoris
crassiorem*. But in all refrainings of anger, it is the best
remedy to win time; and to make a man's self believe,
that the opportunity of his revenge is not yet come, but
that he foresees a time for it; and so to still himself in
the mean time, and reserve it.

To contain anger from mischief, though it take hold
of a man, there be two things whereof you must have
special caution. The one, of extreme bitterness of
words; especially if they be aculeate and proper; for
communia maledicta are nothing so much: and again, that
in anger a man reveal no secrets; for that makes him
not fit for society. The other, that you do not per-
emptorily break off, in any business, in a fit of anger;
but howsoever you shew bitterness, do not act any thing
that is not revocable.

For raising and appeasing anger in another; it is
done chiefly by choosing of times, when men are fro-
wardest and worst disposed, to incense them. Again,
by gathering (as was touched before) all that you can
find out, to aggravate the contempt. And the two
remedies are by the contraries. The former, to take
good times, when first to relate to a man an angry
business; for the first impression is much. And the
other is, to sever, as much as may be, the construction
of the injury from the point of contempt; imputing it
to misunderstanding, fear, passion, or what you will.

Essay LVIII.—OF VICISSITUDE OF THINGS

SALOMON saith, *There is no new thing upon the earth. So that as Plato had an imagination, that all knowledge was but remembrance ;* so Salomon giveth his sentence, *that all novelty is but oblivion.* Whereby you may see that the river of Lethe runneth as well above ground as below. There is an abstruse astrologer that saith, *if it were not for two things that are constant (the one is, that the fixed stars ever stand at like distance one from another, and never come nearer together, nor go further asunder ; the other, that the diurnal motion perpetually keepeth time), no individual would last one moment.* Certain it is, that the matter is in a perpetual flux, and never at a stay. The great winding-sheets, that bury all things in oblivion, are two: deluges and earthquakes. As for conflagrations and great droughts, they do not merely dispeople and destroy. Phaëton's car went but a day. And the three years' drought in the time of Elias was but particular, and left people alive. As for the great burnings by lightnings, which are often in the West Indies, they are but narrow. But in the other two destructions, by deluge and earthquake, it is further to be noted, that the remnant of people which hap to be reserved are commonly ignorant and mountainous people, that can give no account of the time past; so that the oblivion is all one as if none had been left. If you consider well of the people of the West Indies, it is very probable that they are a newer or a younger people than the people of the old world. And it is much more likely that the destruction that hath heretofore been there was not by earthquakes (as the Ægyptian priest told Solon, concerning the island of Atlantis, *that it was swallowed by an earthquake*), but rather that it was desolated by a particular deluge. For earthquakes are

Of Vicissitude of Things

seldom in those parts. But on the other side, they have such pouring rivers, as the rivers of Asia and Africa and Europe are but brooks to them. Their Andes likewise, or mountains, are far higher than those with us; whereby it seems that the remnants of generation of men were, in such a particular deluge, saved. As for the observation that Machiavel hath, that the jealousy of sects doth much extinguish the memory of things; traducing Gregory the Great, that he did what in him lay to extinguish all heathen antiquities; I do not find that those zeals do any great effects, nor last long: as it appeared in the succession of Sabinian, who did revive the former antiquities.

The vicissitude or mutations in the superior globe are no fit matter for this present argument. It may be, Plato's *Great Year*, if the world should last so long, would have some effect; not in renewing the state of like individuals (for that is the fume of those that conceive the celestial bodies have more accurate influences upon these things below than indeed they have), but in gross. Comets, out of question, have likewise power and effect over the gross and mass of things: but they are rather gazed upon and waited upon in their journey, than wisely observed in their effects; specially in their respective effects; that is, what kind of comet, for magnitude, colour, version of the beams, placing in the region of heaven, or lasting, produceth what kind of effects.

There is a toy which I have heard, and I would not have it given over, but waited upon a little. They say it is observed in the Low Countries (I know not in what part) that every five and thirty years the same kind and suit of years and weathers comes about again; as great frosts, great wet, great droughts, warm winters, summers with little heat, and the like; and they call it the *Prime*. It is a thing I do the rather mention, because, computing backwards, I have found some concurrence.

But to leave these points of nature, and to come to men. The greatest vicissitude of things amongst men is the vicissitude of sects and religions. For those orbs rule in men's minds most. The true religion is *built upon the rock;* the rest are tossed upon the waves of time. To speak therefore of the causes of new sects, and to give some counsel concerning them, as far as the weakness of human judgement can give stay to so great revolutions.

When the religion formerly received is rent by discords; and when the holiness of the professors of religion is decayed and full of scandal; and withal the times be stupid, ignorant, and barbarous; you may doubt the springing up of a new sect; if then also there should arise any extravagant and strange spirit to make himself author thereof. All which points held, when Mahomet published his law. If a new sect have not two properties, fear it not; for it will not spread. The one is, the supplanting or the opposing of authority established; for nothing is more popular than that. The other is, the giving licence to pleasures and a voluptuous life. For as for speculative heresies (such as were in ancient times the Arians', and now the Arminians'), though they work mightily upon men's wits, yet they do not produce any great alterations in states, except it be by the help of civil occasions. There be three manner of plantations of new sects: by the power of signs and miracles; by the eloquence and wisdom of speech and persuasion; and by the sword. For martyrdoms, I reckon them amongst miracles; because they seem to exceed the strength of human nature: and I may do the like of superlative and admirable holiness of life. Surely there is no better way to stop the rising of new sects and schisms, than to reform abuses; to compound the smaller differences; to proceed mildly, and not with sanguinary persecutions; and rather to take off the principal authors by winning and advancing them, than to enrage them by violence and bitterness.

The changes and vicissitude in wars are many; but chiefly in three things: in the seats or stages of the war; in the weapons; and in the manner of the conduct. Wars, in ancient time, seemed more to move

Of Vicissitude of Things

from east to west; for the Persians, Assyrians, Arabians, Tartars, (which were the invaders), were all eastern people. It is true, the Gauls were western; but we read but of two incursions of theirs; the one to Gallo-Græcia, the other to Rome. But East and West have no certain points of heaven; and no more have the wars, either from the east or west, any certainty of observation. But North and South are fixed; and it hath seldom or never been seen that the far southern people have invaded the northern, but contrariwise. Whereby it is manifest that the northern tract of the world is in nature the more martial region: be it in respect of the stars of that hemisphere; or of the great continents that are upon the north, whereas the south part, for ought that is known, is almost all sea; or (which is most apparent) of the cold of the northern parts, which is that which, without aid of discipline, doth make the bodies hardest and the courages warmest.

Upon the breaking and shivering of a great state and empire, you may be sure to have wars. For great empires, while they stand, do enervate and destroy the forces of the natives which they have subdued, resting upon their own protecting forces; and then, when they fail also, all goes to ruin, and they become a prey. So was it in the decay of the Roman empire; and likewise in the empire of Almaigne, after Charles the Great, every bird taking a feather; and were not unlike to befall to Spain, if it should break. The great accessions and unions of kingdoms do likewise stir up wars. For when a state grows to an over-power, it is like a great flood, that will be sure to overflow. As it hath been seen in the states of Rome, Turkey, Spain, and others. Look when the world hath fewest barbarous peoples, but such as commonly will not marry or generate, except they know means to live, (as it is almost everywhere at this day, except Tartary), there is no danger of inundations of people: but when there be great shoals of people, which go on to populate without foreseeing means of life and sustentation, it is of necessity that once in an age or two they discharge a portion of their people upon other nations: which the ancient northern people were wont to do by lot; casting lots what part should stay at home, and what should seek their fortunes. When a war-like state grows soft and effeminate, they may be sure of a war. For commonly such states are grown rich in the time of their degenerating; and so the prey inviteth, and their decay in valour encourageth a war.

As for the weapons, it hardly falleth under rule and observation: yet we see even they have returns and vicissitudes. For certain it is, that ordnance was known in the city of the Oxidrakes in India; and was that which the Macedonians called thunder and lightning, and magic. And it is well known that the use of ordnance hath been in China above 2000 years. The conditions of weapons and their improvement are: first, the fetching afar off; for that outruns the danger; as it is seen in ordnance and muskets. Secondly, the strength of the percussion; wherein likewise ordnance do exceed all arietations and ancient inventions. The third is, the commodious use of them: as that they may serve in all weathers; that the carriage may be light and manageable; and the like.

For the conduct of the war: at the first, men rested extremely upon number: they did put the wars likewise upon main force and valour; pointing days for pitched fields, and so trying it out upon an even match: and they were more ignorant in ranging and arraying their battles. After they grew to rest upon number rather competent than vast: they grew to advantages of place, cunning diversions, and the like: and they grew more skilful in the ordering of their battles.

In the youth of a state, arms do flourish: in the middle age of a state, learning; and then both of them together for a time: in the declining age of a state, mechanical arts and merchandize. Learning hath his infancy, when it is but beginning and almost childish: then his youth, when it is luxuriant and juvenile: then his strength of years, when it is solid and reduced: and

Of Vicissitude of Things

lastly, his old age, when it waxeth dry and exhaust. But it is not good to look too long upon these turning wheels of vicissitude, lest we become giddy. As for the philology of them, that is but a circle of tales, and therefore not fit for this writing.

A Fragment of an Essay.—OF FAME

THE poets made Fame a monster. They describe her in part finely and elegantly; and in part gravely and sententiously. They say, look how many feathers she hath, so many eyes she hath underneath; so many tongues; so many voices; she pricks up so many ears.

This is a flourish: there follow excellent parables; as that she gathereth strength in going; that she goeth upon the ground, and yet hideth her head in the clouds; that in the day time she sitteth in a watch tower, and flieth most by night; that she mingleth things done with things not done; and that she is a terror to great cities. But that which passeth all the rest is: they do recount that the Earth, mother of the Giants, that made war against Jupiter and were by him destroyed, thereupon, in an anger, brought forth Fame: for certain it is, that rebels, figured by the Giants, and seditious fames and libels, are but brothers and sisters, masculine and feminine. But now, if a man can tame this monster, and bring her to feed at the hand, and govern her, and with her fly other ravening fowl and kill them, it is somewhat worth. But we are infected with the style of the poets. To speak now in a sad and serious manner: there is not, in all the politics, a place less handled, and more worthy to be handled, than this of fame. We will therefore speak of these points: what are false fames, and what are true fames, and how they may be best discerned; how fames may be sown and raised, how they may be spread and multiplied, and how they may be checked and laid dead; and other things concerning the nature of fame. Fame is of that force, as there is scarcely any great action wherein it hath not a great part; especially in the war. Mucianus undid Vitellius by a fame that he scattered, that Vitellius had in purpose to remove the legions of Syria into

Of Fame

Germany, and the legions of Germany into Syria: whereupon the legions of Syria were infinitely inflamed. Julius Cæsar took Pompey unprovided, and laid asleep his industry and preparations, by a fame that he cunningly gave out, how Cæsar's own soldiers loved him not, and, being wearied with the wars and laden with the spoils of Gaul, would forsake him as soon as he came into Italy. Livia settled all things for the succession of her son Tiberius, by continual giving out that her husband Augustus was upon recovery and amendment. And it is an usual thing with the bashaws, to conceal the death of the Great Turk from the janizaries and men of war, to save the sacking of Constantinople and other towns, as their manner is. Themistocles made Xerxes, king of Persia, post apace out of Græcia, by giving out that the Grecians had a purpose to break his bridge of ships which he had made athwart Hellespont. There be a thousand such like examples; and the more they are, the less they need to be repeated; because a man meeteth with them every where. Therefore let all wise governors have as great a watch and care over fames, as they have of the actions and designs themselves.

The rest was not finished.

INDEX OF QUOTATIONS AND FOREIGN PHRASES

WITH TRANSLATION

The figures in brackets refer to the pages.

Abeunt studia in mores (151): Studies pass into [*i.e.* go to form] character.

Adeste, si, etc. (7): Come now, if anything remains for me to do.

Amici curiæ . . . parasiti curiæ (164): "friends of the court" . . . parasites of the court.

Animasque in vulnere (166): And leave their lives ["souls"] in the wound.

At domus, etc. (110): But the house of Æneas shall rule over all the coasts—his children's children, and those that shall be born of them.

Atque is habitus, etc. (48): The temper of men's minds was such, that while only a few dared to do so vile a deed, many desired it and all acquiesced in it.

Cæsarem portas (122): You carry Cæsar and his fortune.

Cogita quam diu, etc. (6): Consider how long you have been doing the same things: death may be desired not only by the valiant or the miserable, but also by the victim of ennui.

Communia maledicta (167): ill words applicable to all and sundry.

Concessum propter duritiem cordis (123): a thing allowed on account of the hardness of men's hearts. (*Cf.* S. Matt. xix. 8.)

Conflatâ magnâ invidiâ (42): When great ill-will has been conceived [towards a ruler], all his acts, good or bad, alike condemn him.

Consilium Pompeii (96): Pompey follows a truly Themistoclean policy: he thinks that he who commands the sea, commands all.

Cum non sis, etc. (31): When you are no longer the man you have been, there is no reason why you should wish to live.

Cymini sectores (151), dividers of cummin-seed, "hair-splitters."

De facto (32): as a fact, as an actual possession.

Desemboltura (121): "dexterity, readiness" (so defined in Richard Percyvall's *Bibliotheca Hispanica*, 1591); and adroitness which finds an easy and graceful outlet on all occasions for what it is in a man to do or say.

177

Index of Quotations

Devita profanas, etc. (10): Avoid profane novelties of words and oppositions of science falsely so called.   (1 Tim. vi. 20.)

Dolendi modus (44): There is a limit to grieving, but none to fearing.

Duces belli (161), military leaders.

Ecce in deserto . . . Ecce in penetralibus (8): Behold, he is in the desert. . . .   Behold, he is in the secret chambers.   (S. Matt. xxiv. 26.)

Erant in officio (43): They were full of zeal, and yet rather inclined to discuss than to execute the orders of their officers.

Et conversus Deus (32): And God turned to behold the works which his hands had made, and saw that all were very good.   (Genesis i. 31.)

Extinctus amabitur idem (7): The same man, [an object of ill-will while alive], shall be loved when his light is out.

Faber quisque (121): Every man is the architect of his own fortune.

Feri, si, etc. (7): Strike, if it be for the good of the Roman people.

Fons turbatus, etc. (162): A righteous man being cast in his suit in presence of his adversary, is as a troubled fountain and a corrupt spring.   (Prov. xxv. 26.)

Hæc pro amicitiâ (82): These things, out of regard for our friendship, I have not concealed.

Hinc usura vorax (44): Hence usury rapacious, and interest greedily advancing to the reckoning day, hence credit shaken, and war that was a gain to many.

Hoc agere (65), keep to the business in hand.

Hominem delirum (78): A madman, who wrecks weighty realities on mere verbal subtleties.

Idem manebat (128): He remained the same, when it was no longer becoming to him.

Ignavum fucos pecus (123): The drones, an idle swarm, they banish from their hives.

Illam Terra parens (42): Her did mother Earth, inflamed with wrath against the Gods, bring forth (so runs the story), youngest sister to Cœus and Enceladus.

Ille etiam cæcos, etc. (42): He also [the sun] often gives warning of dark rebellions imminent, of treachery and hidden warfare brewing.

Illi mors gravis (31): Death falls heavy on him, who, too well known to all others, dies to himself unknown.

In illo viro (121): There was in him such strength of body and mind, that in whatever rank he had been born, he would have been likely to win fortune for himself.

Iniquum petas (149): Ask for more than is just, in order to get what is just.

In nocte consilium (65): Night brings counsel.

178

Index of Quotations

In studio rei, etc. (107): In his pursuit of wealth it was plain that he sought, not food for avarice, but an instrument of doing good.

In sudore vultûs alieni (108, 123), in the sweat of another's face.

In sudore vultûs tui (123): In thy sweat of thy face, shalt thou eat thy bread. (Genesis iii. 19.)

In veste varietas (10): Let there be variety in the garment, but no rent or cut.

Invidia festos (28): Envy keeps no holidays.

Ira hominis (12): The wrath of man doth not fulfil the justice of God. (S. James i. 20.)

Jam Tiberium vires, etc. (7): Tiberius was fast losing his bodily strength, but not his gift of dissimulation.

Judicis officium (163): It is a judge's office to inquire not only into the facts of a case, but into the times and occasions thereof.

Jus civitatis (93), the right of citizenship; *jus commercii, etc.*: the right of trading, of marriage, of inheritance, of voting, of holding public office.

Juventutem egit (127): He spent a youth full of errors, nay of madnesses.

Laudando præcipere (156), to instruct by praising.

Legi a se, etc. (47): That his soldiers were levied, not bought.

Liberatores or *salvatores* (161), deliverers or saviours.

Liberius, quam, etc. (43): More freely than was compatible with respect for their rulers.

Livia, conjugii, etc. (7): Farewell, Livia, keep after me the memory of our marriage.

Magna civitas (80): A great city is a great solitude.

Magnificabo (157): I will magnify mine office. (Romans xi. 13.)

Magno conatu nugas (78), [produce] trifles with great effort.

Materiam superabit opus (46): The workmanship will excel the material.

Melior natura (51), a better nature.

Memento quod es, etc. (61): Remember that thou art man.—Remember that thou art a God, or God's vice-gerent.

Mitte ambos (68): Send them both naked before strangers and you shall see.

Multum incola fuit (118): My soul hath been a long sojourner. (Ps. cxx. 6.)

Negotiis pares (89, 161), (men who are) equal to conducting affairs.

Nomen bonum (156): A good name is like a fragrant ointment. (Eccl. vii. 1.)

Non deos vulgi (50): It is not profane to deny the gods of the vulgar; but it is profane to apply to the gods the beliefs of the vulgar.

Index of Quotations

Non est curiosus (25): An inquisitive man is sure to be malevolent also.

Non est jam dicere (50): We cannot now say: As the people, so is the priest. For in fact the people are not so [bad] as the priest.

Non inveniet (64): He shall not find faith on the earth. (S. Luke xviii. 8.) *Cf.* Essay i. p. 4.

Nos scimus (165): We know that the law is good, provided that a man use it lawfully. (1 Tim. i. 8.)

Nunc dimittis (7): S. Luke ii. 29.

Octogesimus octavus (112): Eighty-eight, a year of wonders.

Omnis fama (160): All reputation comes from those who are of a man's household.

Omnium consensu (33): All men deemed him fit for empire—had he never become emperor.

Omnium quæ dixerat (159): He had an art of displaying to advantage all that he said and did.

Optimi consiliarii (65): The best counsellors are the dead.

Optimum elige (21): Choose the best, and custom will make it pleasant and easy.

Optimus ille (117): He best asserts the soul's freedom, who snaps the fetters that gall his breast, and ceases once for all to suffer.

Padre commune (153), common Father, Father of all alike.

Parce, puer (102): Boy, spare the goad, and pull harder at the reins.

Participes curarum (81, 161), associates in their cares.

Patres patriæ (161), fathers of their country.

Perpetui principes (161), princes in perpetuity.

Per saltum (26), at a bound.

Pessimum genus (156), the worst sort of enemies, those that praise you.

Philippis iterum (110): Thou shalt see me again at Philippi.

Placebo (66): "I will please" (Ps. cxvi. 9); "to sing a song of *placebo*" = to flatter, to be complaisant.

Plenus rimarum sum (63): I am full of chinks.

Pluet super eos (163): He shall rain snares upon them. (Ps. xi. 6.)

Poco di matto (121), a little of the fool or madman.

Pompa mortis (6): It is the trappings of death that terrify, rather than death itself.

Primum mobile (43, 52, 153), "the first moveable" or "first moved" (*Paradise Lost*, 3, 483): the tenth sphere or heaven of the old astronomy, which carried round with it in its revolution the lower spheres of the planets and fixed stars.

Principis est (64): A prince's greatest virtue is to know his men.

Propagatores or *propugnatores imperii* (161): Extenders or defenders of empire.

Prudens advertit (71): The wise man takes heed to his own steps; the fool turns aside to deceits. (*Cf.* Prov. xiv. 15.)

Index of Quotations

Pulchrorum autumnus pulcher (129): The autumn of the beautiful is beautiful.

Quam volumus licet (51): Esteem ourselves as we may, Senators, yet we are not superior to the Spaniards in numbers, nor to the Gauls in bodily force, nor to the Carthaginians in cunning, nor to the Greeks in arts, nor, indeed, to the Italians and Latins themselves in the inborn domestic sentiment which belongs to this land and nation; but in piety, and religion, and the one great wisdom—the recognition that all is ruled and ordered by the will of the immortal gods—it is here that we have surpassed all tribes and peoples.

Quanta patimur (26): How great are our sufferings!

Qui de contemnendâ, etc. (158): Men who write books "On the duty of despising Glory" allow their name to appear on the title-page.

Qui festinat (107): He that maketh haste to be rich shall not be innocent. (Prov. xxviii, 20.)

Qui finem vitæ, etc. (7): [A mind] that reckons the close of life one of Nature's boons.

Qui fortiter emungit (163): "The wringing of the nose bringeth forth blood." (Prov. xxx. 33.)

Respondes, altero, etc. (78): You reply—with one eyebrow lifted to your forehead and the other drawn down to your chin—that you are no lover of cruelty.

Salus populi (165): The people's welfare is the supreme law.

Satis magnum (29): We are, one to another, a theatre (or spectacle) ample enough.

Secundum genera (65), by classes.

Se non diversas (70): He said he did not [like Burrus] cherish hopes from opposite quarters, but looked simply to the Emperor's safety.

Serpens nisi serpentem (121): A serpent unless it has eaten a serpent does not become a dragon.

Siete Partidas (161), "Seven Parts" (the title of a Digest of the laws of Spain).

Si vixero (47): If I live, the Roman Empire will have no further need of soldiers.

Solus imperantium (33): Vespasian, alone among the emperors, was changed for the better [by empire].

Solvam cingula regum (43): I will loose the girdles of kings. (Isaiah xlv. 1; *cf.* Job xii. 18.)

Sospetto licentia fede (101): Suspicion gives faith [*i.e.* fidelity] leave to depart [*i.e.* releases it from all obligation].

Species virtutibus similes (156), appearances resembling virtues.

Spretâ conscientiâ (156): in disdain of the other's consciousness [of imperfection].

Sui amantes (73): Lovers of themselves without a rival.

Index of Quotations

Sunt plerumque (58): The desires of princes are commonly vehement and contradictory one to another.

Sylla nescivit (47): Sylla was ignorant of letters, he could not "dictate."

Tanquam unus (153), as one of us. (Genesis iii. 22.)

Tantum religio (11): So great the evils to which religion could prompt.

Telam honoris crassiorem (167), honour of a coarser web.

Terra potens (92): A land mighty in arms and in fertility of soil.

Testamenta et orbos (109): Childless men and their bequests were caught by him as in a net.

Tu quoque, Galba (110): Thou also, Galba, shalt taste of empire.

Ubi peccat, etc. (131): Where she errs in the one, she runs a risk in the other.

Ultima primis cedebant (128): The last of him was not equal to the first.

Ut puto Deus fio (7): Meseems I am becoming a God.

Vena porta (60, 123), the "gate-vein" which distributes blood to the liver.

Venient annis (110): In later ages there shall come a time, when Ocean shall loose the bands of nature, and a vast continent shall lie open, and Tiphys shall disclose new worlds, and Thule shall no longer be the end of the earth.

Ver perpetuum (138), a perpetual Spring.

Versatile ingenium (121), versatility.

Vetulam suam (23): He preferred his old wife to immortality [*i.e.* Penelope to Calypso].

Vinum dæmonum (4), wine of devils.

GLOSSARY

Abatement, the "small matter" deducted for fee to the state, 126.

Abridgement, epitome, 96.

Abroad, put, laid open, spread out, 84.

Absurd, unreasonable, 18, 79, 144. Cf. *absurdly* (which qualifies *pursue*), 127.

Abuses, deceptions, 148. *Abuseth them*, deceives, misleads them (*i.e.* old men), 127. So *abusing*, 71.

Actor, a speaker, 76.

Aculeate, furnished with a sting, pointed, incisive, 167.

Adamant, a magnet or lodestone, 55.

Admittance, by, by admission, as if granted or allowed, 78.

Adust, burnt up, dried up with heat (see *Choler*), 113.

Advancements, gifts, bequests, 109.

Adventures, ventures, risky enterprises, 109. See also *Charge*.

Advised, deliberate, cautious, circumspect, 56, 162.

Advoutresses, adultresses, 59.

Æquinoctia, equinoxes, 42.

Affect, to desire, aim at, aspire to, 1, 25, 37, 70, 79, 160; to like, be fond of, 118. *Affected dispatch*, excessive striving after expedition, 76.

Affection, liking, inclination, 21.

After, afterwards (*e.g.* "After they grew," 172). *After as*, according as, 119.

Aim, taking an, guessing, 53.

Allay, alloy, 4.

Alley = bowling-alley, 68.

Allow, to approve, 54, 79, 155.

Almaigne, Germany, 171.

Almost, for the most part, 129.

Ambassage, embassy, 90. (Cf. *Embassages*.)

Amiable, worthy of love, lovable, 129.

And it were, 73, *and it be*, 122: here *and* = if.

Answered some small matter, guaranteed some small fee, 126.

Antecamera, antechamber, 136.

Antics, buffoons, burlesque performers, 116. (Spelt "Antiques" in the original.)

Antimasque, a comic or burlesque interlude between the acts of a masque, 116.

Apparent, plainly visible, manifest, 121.

183

Glossary

Appetite, in, eager for advancement, 144.

Apply, suit, adapt, 102; *apply oneself to,* adapt or accommodate oneself to, study, 21, 155.

Apposed of, questioned about, 69.

Apprehendeth, intends, means, 146.

Apricocks, apricots, 138.

Arbitrement, arbitration, 9.

Argument, subject or theme for consideration, 89.

Arietations, assaults with the *aries* or battering-ram, 172.

Artificial, artful, skilful, 47.

As often = that; *e.g. so as* = so that, 23, 31, etc.; *so as* = provided that, 77; *that . . . as* = such . . . that, 17, 40, 82, 105, 142; also "it is the nature . . . *as* they will set," 73; "to provide *as,*" 100.

Aspects, the appearance of the planets in regard to their position among the heavenly bodies at a given time; taken here to mean their "gaze" or look upon the earth, 24.

Assured, sure, certain, 33, 44; trusty, 48.

Attained, come up to, equalled in excellence, 74.

Aversation, aversion, 80.

Avoidances, (fine), (skilfully contrived) channels or outlets by which the water may run off, 136.

Band, bond, 8, 43.

Barriers, tilting within barriers or lists, 116.

Battles, battalions, bodies of troops, 172.

Baugh, said to mean the Bass Rock, 111.

Bear it, carry their point, bear the matter out, 78.

Beat over, to: perhaps a metaphor from the hunt, 70, 151.

Beautified, adorned, was an adornment of, 4.

Because, to the end that, in order that, 22, 76, 107.

Become, where to, where to get oneself, 135.

Becomen, become, 93.

Beholding, beholden, indebted, 29, 159.

Bent, bent-grass, reed-grass, 138.

Births, children, offspring, 74.

Blacks, black garments of mourning, 6.

Blanch, flatter, 65; slip away from, shirk, pass over, 78.

Blushing, i.e. such as to cause a blush, 86.

Box, the "bank" in a game of hazard, 124.

Brave, to make a bold show or parade of, 47; *braves,* defies, makes light of, 29. *Brave (commodity),* excellent, 105.

Bravery, ostentation, bravado, boasting, 32, 46, 77, 158; a piece of boastfulness, 166; showiness, splendour, 116; *upon bravery,* out of bravado, 114.

Breaketh, subdues, subjects, trains, 154.

Broke, do business, negotiate, 108.

Glossary

Broken music, probably = concerted music, music written in parts for several instruments, 115.

Bruit, noise, clamour, 158.

Buckling towards, girding oneself to encounter, going to meet, 67.

Bullises, bullaces (wild plums), 138.

Burses, Exchanges, "*Bourses*," 54.

By-ways, indirect ways (for approaching or "getting at" the Court), 164; *cf.* 33.

Can, to, to be able, 31.

Canvasses, intrigues, 68.

Card, chart, 55, 90.

Care not (to innovate), are not cautious (about innovating), 127.

Cast it, contrive, 135. *Casteth them*, makes them incline on one side or other, turns the scale, 153.

Castoreum, a medicine obtained from the beaver, 81.

Cat in the pan, the turning of the: ? reversing the order of things so dexterously as to make them appear the opposite of what they really are (*New English Dict.*), 70.

Catchpole, a sheriff's officer, bailiff, 157. Hence is evolved the phrase, *catching and poling* = snatching and plundering (see *Poling*), 164.

Cauterised, seared (in conscience: see 1 Tim. iv. 2), 50.

Censure, judgment, expression of opinion, 89.

Certain (allowance), fixed, 105.

Certainty, trustworthiness, 17.

Certify, send information, 104.

Cessions, concessions, yielding to another's judgment, 159.

Challenge, claim, 146, 148.

Chamairis, a dwarf iris, 137.

Chapmen, purchasers, customers, 108.

Charge and adventure upon = involving expense and risk, 158.

Chargeable, costly, 95.

Check with, clash with, interfere with, 30, 100.

Choice, with, with discrimination, 38.

Choler, bile, one of the four "humours," supposed to cause irascibility of temper: *choler adust*, "black bile," another of the humours, the cause of melancholy (here recognised as a morbid condition of bile), 113.

Chop with, bandy words with, 164.

Chopping, exchanging, buying and selling again, 108.

Churchmen, clerics, ecclesiastics, 22, 60.

Circumstance, attendant ceremony, accompaniments of an action, 160; *circumstances*, roundabout details, circumlocution, 103.

Civil, orderly, cultivating the arts of peace, 52; orderly, decorous, seemly, 146; *civil shrift*, lay confession, 81.

Civility, civilisation, 137.

Glossary

Clamour, disturb with clamour, 66.

Clear, to free from pecuniary embarrassment, 87.

Close, secret, concealed, 33, 162.

Clove gillyflower, the clove pink, 138.

Coemption, the buying up of the entire supply of any commodity in the market, 109.

Collect, infer, 112.

Collegiate, united as in a college or corporate body, 120.

Colour, to give their own name to (other men's money), *i.e.* to lend it out on usury under their own name, 126.

Come off speedily for the time, make good progress with business in a comparatively short time, 76.

Comeliness, propriety, seemliness, 86.

Comely, becoming, seemly, 159.

Comforteth, strengthens, confirms, 120

Commiserable, deserving pity or commiseration, 106.

Commodity, adventage, 123, 133.

Communicate, shared (*with*), 38.

Compass, kept their, kept within their own bounds, 93.

Composition, blending of qualities in a man's character, temperament, 19, 64, 127.

Conceit, imagination, 107; thought, intellect, 163. *Conceits*, thoughts, ideas, 19.

Concurrence, coincidence or agreement as to dates, 169.

Conference, talk, discussion, 135, 150; so *confer*, converse, 150.

Confidence of, confident belief in, 51; *hath confidence with*, is trusted by, 47.

Conscience, consciousness, 32.

Construction, interpretation, 166, 167.

Contain, hold in, hold together, 93; confine, restrict (*within*), 8, 94; restrain (*from*), 167.

Contend, strive, endeavour, 160.

Content much, give much pleasure, 102.

Conversation, way of life, 80; intercourse, 81. *Converse in*, are engaged in or occupied with, 118, cf. *conversant in*, 65.

Convince, refute, 49.

Copulate, united, linked together, 120.

Cornelian-tree, the cornel-tree, cornelian cherry, 137; *cornelians*, the fruit of this tree, 138.

Correspondence (*good*), comparison, proportion, corresponding position, 48. *With correspondence to, i.e.* in a way which is appropriate to each particular case, 152.

Corroborate, strengthened, reinforced, 119.

Country manners, his, the manners of his own country, 56.

Course, out of, out of order, irregularly, 142.

Crocus vernus, spring crocus, 137.

Cross, run counter to, thwart, 148, 149.

Glossary

Cross clauses, contrary clauses, 9; cf. *cross lies*, 158.
Crossness, disposition to be contrary, perverseness, 38.
Crudities, undigested matter, 76.
Curiosity, elaborate workmanship or design, 141; *curiosities*, nice points, subtleties, 24.
Curious, minutely inquiring, 24; over-careful or scrupulous, 155; over-elaborate, over-subtle, 77, 78; occult, magical (arts), 111.
Curiously, with minute attention, 150.
Currans, currants, 142.
Currently, with ready or easy flow, 100.

Dammasin, damson, 137.
Daubed, loaded with tasteless ornament, 115.
Decay, cause of destruction, "ruin," 114.
Deceivable, apt to deceive, deceptive, 131.
Deceive, cheat, defraud (*i.e.* of nourishment), 142.
Decent, fit, seemly, graceful, 129, 136, 142.
Declination, decline, decay, 70, 94.
Decline, turn aside, avert, 122.
Deduced, brought before a tribunal, 165.
Deliveries, fine, ingenious methods of getting out of or getting rid of (danger), 58. *Deliveries of a man's self,* perhaps = ways of bringing out or giving effect to what is in him, 121.
Denying, refusing, 148. So *denial*, refusal, 149.
Dependences, dependencies, prerogatives, 64; body of dependants, clientèle, 114. *Hath a dependence of,* is dependent upon, 60.
Depraving, slandering, 148.
Derive, turn aside, divert, 27.
Desert, a "wilderness," 139. (See *Heath*.)
Destitute, desert, leave destitute, 106.
Device, the plot or arrangement of a masque or pageant, 115, 116.
Device, point; see *Point device.*
Diet, take his meals, 55.
Difference, subtle distinction, 78.
Difficilness, the character of one who is difficult to deal with, 38.
Direction, wits of, intellects with a gift for directing or deciding affairs, 71.
Disabling, disparaging, depreciating, 148.
Discern (from), distinguish (from), 114, 174.
Discharge itself, free itself from the charge, clear itself, 101.
Discoloured, bereft of colour, pale, 6.
Discommodity, disadvantage, 106, 123, 125, 133.
Discourse high, "talk big," 60.
Discoursing, discursive, passing lightly from one thought to another, 3.
Discover, make known or manifest, disclose, reveal, 16, 145, 147.
Discovery, revelation, disclosure, 18, 123, 149.

Glossary

Dispenseth with, excuses, condones, 113.

Disreputation, bringing into disrepute, 147.

Distasted, disgusted, 148. So *distastes*, annoyances, 15.

Ditty, the words of a song, 115.

Doctor, teacher, 8.

Donative, giving, bestowing, 107; a gift, present, 47, 61, 97.

Doubt, to fear, suspect, think likely, 69, 87, 170.

Dry, hard, severe; *dry blow*, a smart hit, 103.

Dryness, condition of being dried up, failure, 125.

Ease to be, find, find it comfortable to be, 79.

Eccentrics, circles or orbits not having the earth exactly at their centre, 52.

Edge, stimulate, "egg on," 125.

Ejaculation, a darting forth, emission of rays, 24.

Election, choice, discrimination, 147; liberty to choose, option, 131.

Embaseth, debases, makes base, 4, 30.

Embassages, embassies, 157. (Cf. *Ambassage*.)

Embossments, projections, 140.

Employed men, employés, attachés, 55. *Employed to*, used for, 105.

Engaged (*with*), bound, stuck fast in, 120.

Engines, contrivances, "machinery," 52, machines, 119.

Engrossing, monopolising, 26, 46.

Ensigns, insignia, decorations, 97.

Entertainment, something to occupy or divert men's thoughts, 148.

Epicure, Epicurean, follower of Epicurus, 11.

Epicycle, a little circle, whose centre describes a greater circle (*eccentric*) about the earth; each of the planets was supposed to move in such a small circle (52).

Equality of bores, ? pipes of equal bore (*i.e.* equal to that of the "spouts"), 141.

Equipollent, equal in power, equivalent, 119.

Espials, spies, 146. (Cf. *Spials*.)

Estate, a State, government, 28, 40, 165, Essay xxix., etc.; so *business of estate, matters of estate* (= State affairs), 65, 89, 165; *discourse of estate*, 68.—*His own estate*, his own affairs, 24.— *Estates of men* = orders, professions, 146.

Estivation, passing the summer: *place of estivation* = a summer retreat, 136.

Evil-favoured: see *Favour*.

Exaltation, in his, in the region where its influence is strongest (a term of astrology), 120.

Excusations, excuses, making excuses, 77, 159.

Exercised, practised and disciplined in the battle of life, 122.

Exhaust, exhausted, 23, 173.

Expect, wait for, 108.

Glossary

Experience, trial, experiment: *would be put in experience* = ought to be tried, 105.

Expert men, men who have been trained by experience or practice, 150.

Extern, external, outside, 128.

Facile, easily wrought upon or "got at," 22. *Facility*, undue readiness to please, give way to, or be swayed by others, 32, 33, 38, 155.

Facts, deeds, acts, 12.

Fair, in parenthesis = just, simply: *i.e.* "will e'en let him go on," 19.

Fall under, admit of, 90, 172. *Falleth upon that*, notes the fact, 121.

Falls, ? incidents, incidental passages (of affairs); or perhaps issues, conclusions, 71.

Fame, rumour, report, 42, 174, 175; reputation, 19, 158, 159.

Fashions, a man's habits or "ways," 145.

Fast, tenacious, retentive ("of their smells"), 138.

Fast upon, close upon, 40.

Favour, features, expression of the countenance, 85, 129. *Evil-favoured*, ill-looking, "ugly," 119.

Fearful, timid, 89, 114; *fearfulness*, timidity, 19.

Feeding humours, ministering to a superior's caprices, 109; cf. *feed his humour*, 64.

Feigned prices, "fancy prices," 107.

Fetching, reaching, striking, 172.

Fifth essence = quintessence, the immutable essence of which the heavenly bodies are formed, 49.

Figure, in, so as to form a pattern, as a complete picture, 84. Cf. *turning . . . into figure*, 115.

Filberds, filberts, 138.

Final to, have been, have put an end to, 96.

Flags, insignia, 40.

Flash, for a, for a moment, 94.

Flashy, insipid, "flat," 150.

Flos Africanus, a kind of marigold, 138.

Flower-delices, irises (*fleurs-de-lis*), 138.

Fly, fly at (with a hawk), 174.

Foot, under; see *Under*.

Foot-pace, a raised floor or platform (on which the bench is set), 164.

Foresee, provide, 45, 136, 171.

Forth, go, go on, proceed (in his speech), 69.

Forwardness, in, making progress, 106, 149.

Forwards, forward, eager, 56.

Frame, out of, disordered, out of gear, 43.

Freely, without charge, gratis, 123.

Frairly, friar-like, 107.

Fritillaria, fritillary, 137.

189

Glossary

From (the sun), turned from, away from, 135.

Fume, empty fancy, 169.

Futile, incontinent of speech, talkative, 18, 63.

Galliard, an old French dance of a spirited character, 103.

Gallo-Græcia, Galatia, 171.

Gaudery, showy display, 97.

Gingles, jingles, rattles, 106.

Ginnitings, jennetings (a kind of early apple), 138.

Given over, given up, abandoned, 160, 169.

Globe, a complete or perfect body of things, 32.

Glorious, ostentatious, vain-glorious, 109, 146, 158, 159.

Glory, vain-glory, 158, 163; fine show, splendour, 115, 116.

Goeth away with it, wins the advantage, comes off the winner, 153.

Grace, favour, 81.   *Grace themselves*, do themselves credit, 144.

Gracing, complimenting, 164.

Gracious, acceptable to others, deserving their thanks, 148; graceful, 129, 159.

Graze, to, to be grown with grass (*i.e.* the four quarters of the court divided by paths running across at right angles, are to be laid with turf), 135.

Great with, so, on such intimate terms with, 147.

Great Year, Plato's, a great cycle of years, at the end of which the celestial bodies would be found to have returned to the positions they were in at the beginning of the cycle, 169.

Grotta, grotto, 136.

Ground, underlying rule or principle, 132.

Grounds of several natures, different kinds of soil, 133.

Growing silk, ? vegetable silk, "grass silk," 105.

Haberdashers of small wares, retail dealers or vendors, 68.

Habilitation, qualification, a making apt or able, 94.

Half piece, as an, imperfect, wanting the other half, 82.

Hand, at a dear, at a dear rate, 76.   *Of even hand*, at an even balance (of accounts, *i.e.* not having a balance "on the wrong side"), 87.   *To come at even hand*, to come to an equality, to be even (with another), 24.

Hap, happen, chance, 168.

Healths, the drinking of healths or toasts (which, in Bacon's time, meant deep drinking), 55.   (*Cf.* 117.)

Hearken how they waste, ascertain how their numbers dwindle, 106.

Hearse-like, funereal, 15.

Heath, part of a garden left in a wild state, "wilderness," 139, 140, 141.

Herba muscaria, grape-hyacinth, 138.

Hierusalem, Jerusalem, 104.

Hold out, keep up, continue on (that scale), 147.

Hollyokes, hollyhocks, 138.

Holpen, helped, 64, 74, 89.

Glossary

Hooded, having the head covered up so that they cannot see (a term of falconry), 54.

Hortatives, exhortations, 23.

Humorous, guided by one's own "humour," full of odd "humours," or fancies, 22.

Hyacinthus orientalis, the ordinary cultivated hyacinth, 137.

Impertinency, irrelevance, 163.   *Impertinent*, irrelevant, 78.

Importeth, is of importance, 9, 90, 94.

Importune, importunate, 28, 117, 146.

Impostumations, impostumes, abscesses, 46.

Impression, of the last, under the influence of what they have been last impressed by, 147.

Imprinting, impressive, 154.

Impropriate, appropriate, 97.

Inbowed windows, bow-windows, 135.

Incensed, burnt (as incense), 16.

Incommodities, disadvantages, drawbacks, 123.

Inconformity, incongruity, 74.

Incurreth . . . into the note, comes under the observation (of others), 25.

Indifferent, impartial, 18, 40, 65, 152.

Industriously, purposely, 18.

Infamed, made infamous, 59.

Information, make an, make something known, bring something to the notice of others, 148.

Infortunate, unfortunate, 14, 122.

Inordinate, ungoverned (in one's passions), 29.

Intend, to be bent on, to devote oneself to, 69, 94 (so *intention*, same passage); to mean, signify, 62.

Interessed, interested, 12.

Interest; to have interest in (a person), to have influence with him, to be able to influence him, 145, 158.

Interest at, i.e. on terms for which they would have to pay heavily later on, 59.

Interlocution, speaking turn and turn about with others, 103.

Intervenient, intervening, 165.

Inure, to train, habituate, 114.

Inward, intimate, confident, 33, 64.   *Inward beggar, i.e.* a secret bankrupt, concealing his poverty, 79.

Jade, to over-drive, 102.

Just (cure), proper, exact, 45.

Justs, jousts, tilting with the lance, 116.

Kind, in that, in that way, 18, 125.   Cf. *in some other kind*, 85.

Knap, hillock, knoll, 133.

Glossary

Knee-timber, timber that is bent or grown crooked, 38.
Knots, garden beds, plots, 139.

Laudatives, eulogies, 96.
Lay (buried), lie, 118.
Leads, a goodly, a handsome leaded roof, 134.   (*Cf. leaded aloft*, 136.)
Leese, lose, 60, 89, 100, 104.
Legend, the Golden Legend (*Legenda aurea*), or collection of Lives
    of the Saints, compiled in the thirteenth century by Jacobus de
    Voragine, 49.
Letter, letter of recommendation, 149.
Letting, for, for fear of hindering or obstructing, 140.
Life, the, the reality, the persons as they actually live, 55.   *To life*,
    to the life, vividly, 85.
Light well, fall to a worthy possessor, 130.
Lightly, usually, 153.
Like, likely, 69 (and elsewhere).
Lilium convallium, lily of the valley, 138, 141.
Limited, determined, measured, 87.
Lively, livelily, vividly, 15.
Loading part, on the, on the side which adds to the load or weight
    (and so aggravating the misfortune), 38.
Look: used to call attention or give emphasis to the statement that
    follows, 156, 171.
Looses (in the conclusion), ways out of difficult or "tight" places, 71.
Lot, the spell cast by witchcraft or sorcery, 27.
Lurcheth, swallows up, absorbs, 133.

Main, the body of a thing, the chief or principal part (? = main
    stream), 71.
Mainly, strongly, greatly, 43, 108.
Maintain, support, back, 82; so *maintained*, 51.
Make for, to be conducive to, 3, 95; *for whom it maketh*, for whose
    advantage it is, 49.   *Make forth to*, advance towards, 123.
    Make good, justify, 23.
Manage, management, 127.
Managed well, properly broken and trained (in the manège), well
    in hand, 17.
Manure, to till or cultivate, 105.
Many times, often, in many cases, 18, 20, 21, 23, 42, 46, 67, 73,
    129, 152.
Marish, marshy, 106.
Masteries, superiority (over disease), superior strength, 99; *to try
    masteries with*, to contend with for victory, to measure one's
    strength against, 58.
Mate, to overpower, 6, 44.
Material, dealing nakedly and abruptly with the real matter in
    hand (without preface or circumlocution), 77.

Glossary

Matted pink, a small creeping pink, used for borders, 138.

Matter the: (we now omit the definite article), 4, 168.

Matter, upon the, all things considered, on the whole, 131.

May, ? the Isle of May in the Firth of Forth, 111.

Mean, means (to an end), instrument, agency, 58, 148, 149. *In a mean*, in moderate terms or language, 15.

Meere stone, a boundary stone, 162.

Meeteth with it, answers it, hits the point, 80.

Melocotones, a large kind of peach, 138.

Mercury rod, the caduceus, borne by Mercury when he conducts the shades of the dead to Hades, 12.

Merely, absolutely, entirely, 9, 96, 168.

Mew, to moult, 91.

Militar, military, 158.

Militia, an army, soldiery, 91, 93.

Mintmen, men versed in coinage, 65.

Model, the plan of a work, the scale on which it is made or done, 10, 134, 143; *little model*, a frame or plan in little, 97; *after the model of*, proportionate to, on the scale of, 72.

Moderator, a chairman or president (at a debate or other proceedings), 76. *Moderate*, act as moderator, control the talk, 102.

Moil, labour, 105.

Momus, in the fable, found fault with a house for not being built on wheels, so that its occupant might get away from bad neighbours, 133.

Morris dance, a dance of mummers on May-day, 9.

Mought, might, 46, 68, 82, 108, 112.

Muniting, fortifying, 10.

Mystery, secret or hidden meaning, 15. *Mysteries are due to secrecy: i.e.* the man who can keep silence is the right person to impart mysteries to, 18.

Naught, bad, evil, worthless, 108, 156.

Nephews, grandsons, 82.

Newel, the central column of a winding staircase; where the steps are pinned into the wall and there is no central pillar, the staircase is said to have an *open newel* (134).

Nice, scrupulous, "particular," 92; *nice or dainty*, over-delicate or "pretty," 115.

Niceness, fastidiousness, 6.

Note, notice, 25; *are in note*, are noticed or observed, 154; something notified, information, 149.

Nourish little, receive little nourishment, 60.

Obnoxious, exposed, liable, or subject (*to*), 65, 114; submissive, 131.

Obtain, attain (*to*), 17; *obtaineth*, prevails, wins its cause, 164.

Odds, eminent, marked advantage or superiority, 146.

Oes, small round discs or "spangles" (like the letter O), 115.

Glossary

Of long, for long, 163.

Officious, forward to do offices, ready to serve, 131, 146.

Opinion, reputation, credit, 79, 158, 160; *to have openness in fame and opinion, i.e.* to have a reputation for frankness, 19; *opinion of the touch of a man's reputation, i.e.* the belief that one's reputation is touched or attacked, 167.

Orbs, spheres, 43, 153; orbits, 52.

Ought, aught, anything, 171.

Overcome, become master of, make one's own, 108.

Over-speaking, addicted to over-much speaking, 163.

Owing a man, etc.: = which he will have to pay for in old age, 98.

Pack the cards, arrange or shuffle the cards fraudulently to the advantage of one's own hand, 68.

Pairs, impairs, 74.

Palm, a hand's-breath, 58.

Pardon, by, by making allowances, 129.

Particular, partial, 168, 169. (*In his own*) *particular* = particular case or affairs, 47.

Passable, of tolerable ability, 146; *passable with*, acceptable to, 152.

Passages, ? the connecting portions of a speech, serving for transition from one topic to another, 77.

Passport, leave of departure, 101.

Paul's, St. Paul's Cathedral or " Paul's Walk," used as a general promenade and place of resort in Bacon's time, 70.

Pawns, pledges, 124.

Perfect in, skilled or accomplished in, 68, 155.

Period, termination, conclusion, 76, 128.

Perish, cause to perish, injure, 83.

Personal, awarded to individuals, 96.

Personate, to assign a part or character to, 11.

Philology, the literature of a subject, 173.

Piece, fit in (as one piece), 74. *Pieced* (*up*), patched up, 10, 106.

Pine-apple trees, pine-trees, 137.

Piony, peony, 137.

Place, precedence, 55; a topic, 174. *To take little place*, to have but small weight or effect, 149.

Placebo; see Index of Phrases.

Plant, to colonise; *plantation*, a colony, colonising, 104–6.

Platform, outline or general plan, 142.

Plausible, praiseworthy, deserving applause, 27, 42.

Play-pleasure, the pleasure felt in witnessing a play or drama, 24.

Pleasing, complaisant, 99.

Ply, a bend (given to the mind: cf. *pliant* just before), 120.

Point, a subject or matter (defined by what follows): thus, *point of estate* = the State, something that concerns the State, 165; *from the point of contempt, i.e.* from any implication of contempt, 167.

194

Glossary

Point, to appoint, 135, 172.

Point device, fashioned or adjusted with extreme precision, 155.

Politic (spelt *politique* and *politicke* in orig. edition), political, belonging to or concerned with the State: *politic person* or *man* = politician, 26, 67; *politic ministers* = ministers of State, 95; *politic body* = body politic, the State, 35, 95.

Politics, politicians, statesmen, 9, 17, 38.

Politics, the, the science of politics or statecraft, 174.

Poll, a "head" or unit of population; *the hundred* (= hundredth) *poll*, *i.e.* one man in a hundred, 91.

Poller, one who exacts money, 165.

Polling, plundering, exacting fees, 164. (See *Catchpole*.)

Popular, courting the favour of the people, 48; so *popularity*, 146.

Poser, an examiner or questioner in the Schools, 103.

Practice, plotting, intrigue, crafty dealing, 11, 68, 108, 145.

Praying in aid of alchymists, calling in alchemists to help the case, 83.

Precisely, look, keep a keen watch, 124.

Pre-occupateth, anticipates, 6.

Prescription, title (to be considered lucky), 144.

Present, a formal message or injunction, 94.

Present wit, a ready mind, 151.

Presently, straightway, immediately, 85, 124.

Presseth, depresses, 40.

Prest, prompt, 95.

Pretendeth, makes a pretext of, 75; *cf.* 94, *as may be pretended*.

Prevent, anticipate, 163.

Pricked, planted, 141; so perhaps *prick in*, 56.

Primum mobile; see Index of Phrases.

Principal, initial, 111.

Private, for his own; i.e. private benefit, 105.

Proceeder, small, one who makes small progress, 117.

Proof, the result of trial or experience: *the proof is best* = it is found to turn out best, 20.

Proper (of words), having a personal application, 167.

Propriety, special character, 8.

Prospectives, "perspective glasses," an optical contrivance of the stereoscope-kind, 78.

Proyning, cultivating, pruning, 150.

Purchase, to obtain, acquire, 13, 160; *a new purchase*, a new acquisition, 153.

Purchasing, acquisition of landed property, 124.

Pure, free (of inhabitants), unoccupied, 104.

Purpose of, intentionally, purposely, 27.

Purprise, enclosure, enclosed area, 164.

Pursuit, pursuit of office, canvassing, 81.

Push, pustule, blister, 157.

Glossary

Put you in way for, put you in the way of, 85.

Puzzle, distraction, 31.

Pyramides, pyramids (the Latin pl.: elsewhere Bacon uses the sing. *pyramis*), 140.

Pythonissa, a woman possessed with a spirit of divination, 110.

Quadlins, codlins, 138.

Quarrel, reason, plea, 23; cf. *grounds and quarrels*, 95.

Quarter, keep, keep its proper place, 30; *kept good quarter between themselves*, kept on friendly terms, 70.

Queching = either (1) flinching or (2) crying out, 119.

Quicken, give life to, stimulate, 125, 144, 149.

Quickest, most vivid, 160.

Quire, choir, 115.

Race, the extent to which a thing goes, 166.

Rasps, raspberries, 138.

Ravisheth, carries away violently or hastily, 52.

Reason (*it is, it were*), reasonable, 22, 31, 41. *Much like is the reason of* = their case is much the same, 132.

Recamera, inner chamber, back chamber, 136.

Receipt, receptacle, 140; recipe, prescription, 81, 84, 151.

Reciproque, reciprocal; *the reciproque* = reciprocal affection, 30.

Reduce, carry back, trace up, 32.

Reduced, brought within limits, 172.

Referendaries, referees, 148.

Regard upon = out of personal regard, 155. *In regard*, because, 92.

Regiment, regimen, Essay xxx.

Reiglement, regulation, 125.

Relate himself, tell his thoughts, 84.

Remover, one who is always moving about or stirring, 122.

Reparation of a denial: the gaining of one's suit, on a second urging, after it has been once refused, 149.

Reputed of, well, having a good reputation, 48.

Resemblance, comparison, likening, 165; *resembled*, likened, compared, 53.

Resorts, ? springs, starting-points, sources; or = the springs or movements (of machinery), 71.

Respect, have regard to, 99. *Respected*, attended to, 20. *Respects*, regard for persons, personal considerations, punctilious observances, 33, 40, 155; Essay lii. (title). *In respect*, in case, 87. *In respect of*, in comparison with, as compared with, 96, 122.

Rest, set up their, staked everything (upon an issue), 96.

Restrained, confined, restricted (*to*), 84, 126.

Returns, wings or side-buildings built out at the back of a house, 134. *The row of return*, the line of these buildings, on either side of the "court," 135.

Glossary

Ribes, currants, 138.

Rid, dispatch, get done, 93.

Rise, though it be of the best, i.e. come from the best source, 109.

Rise in his suit, *i.e.* begin by asking little, and gradually increase his demands, 149.

Round (dealing), straightforward, direct, 4; *spoil the feathers of round flying, i.e.* prevent their flying direct to the mark, 19.

Sad, sober, 174; of sober hue, 16.

Sarza, sarsaparilla, 80.

Satyrian, a species of orchis, 138.

Scantling, measure, limit, 161.

Scope, aim, object aimed at, 94.

Season, in, in their happy time, at the time when they come out strongest, 38.

Secure, without care, at ease, 44; *security*, serene freedom from care, sense of safety, 15.

Seek for, to, at a loss for, 125.

Seeled, having the eyelids sewn up (a term of falconry), 113.

Seelings, panellings, wainscotings, 159.

Sensible (of), sensitive *(to)*, 22, 34, 95, 114, 166.

Sentence, judgment, opinion, 168.

Several, separate, distinct, different, 17, 61, 133, 134, 152.

Severally, differently, 134.

Sharings, partnerships, 108.

Shrewd, mischievous, hurtful, 72.

Shut itself out to take, debar itself from taking, 125.

Side (oneself), to take a side, adhere to one party, 33, 153.

Slide, smoothness of motion, 41, 122.

Slight it over, dismiss it slightly, slur it over, 36.

Slope, sloping, 140.

Slug, drag, hindrance to motion, 124.

Smother, pass in, be smothered or stifled, 84; cf. *keep in smother*, 100.

Soap-ashes, alkalis, 105.

Softly, with slow or gentle movement, 17, 43.

Solecism, a gross error or blunder, 58.

Sort with, agree or harmonise with, match, suit, 17, 86, 118; associate or consort with, 20; *sorteth to*, turns to, results in, 21, 81; *it sorted with them*, things turned out in their case, they feared (accordingly), 93.

Spaces, intervals, 118.

Spangs, spangles, 115.

Speculative into, disposed to pry into, 64.

Spials, spies, 131. (Cf. *Espials*.)

Spirits, good, men of good or noble spirit, **7**.

Spoken to, spoken upon, discussed, 65.

Glossary

Sponne, spun, 111.

Staddles, young trees left standing in a copse when other trees and underwood are cut down, 91.

Stages, the "theatre" of wars, 170.

State, an estate, 88, 109; government, statecraft, 98; a rank or order of persons, 60 (of the clergy), 92. (Cf. *Estate*.)

State, to keep, to observe some degree of formality, to be dignified, 154.

Stately, statelily, in stately manner, 3, 137.

Statua, statue, 84; *statuas*, 116, 134, 136, 141, 143.

Stay at a, at rest, 168; *stand at a stay*, stand still, 36, 41, 57; *give stay to*, arrest the progress of, 170.

Steal it, do it stealthily, 33.

Stick, hesitate, scruple, 70, 162.

Stirps, stocks, families, 40.

Stond, impediment, stoppage, 121, 151.

Stood upon, insisted upon, 94.

Store, a good quantity, 105, 106.

Stoved, kept in a hothouse, 137.

Success, result, issue, 144, 148.

Sufficiency, ability, 33, 62, 78, 79, 146, 161. *Sufficient*, able, competent, capable, 89, 155.

Suit, "suite," sequence, 169.

Surcharge, excess of population (greater than the land will support), 106.

Suspect, suspicious, 153; *a suspect*, an object for suspicion, 75, 156.

Sustentation, sustenance, 171.

Take (*the sense*), charm (the feelings or judgment), 115. *Take in with* = take up with, join, 153. *Take with*, take, admit, employ, 146. *Take a fall*, suffer a defeat, 19. *Take up*, purchase, 59.

Tarrasses, terraces, 136.

Taxing, censuring, finding fault with, 32.

Temperature, temperament, 19.

Tendering, treating with care, nursing, 99.

Terms, upon, *i.e.* on terms of formality, 86.

That = that which, what: *e.g.* "that he is not *that* he is," (18); "of *that* you are thought to know, ... *that* you know not," (103); "to see *that* it cannot perfectly discern," (115); "seem to know *that* he doth not" (*i.e.* what he doth not know), (151); "upon *that* it falls" (= that which it falls upon), (166).

Theatre, spectacle, assemblage of things presented to the view, 32.

Theologues, theologians, 157.

Thorough, through, 15, 135, 139.

Throughly, thoroughly, 49, 166.

Touch, speech of, speech that has a direct personal reference (and "comes home to a man"), 103. (See also s. v. *Opinion*.)

Glossary

Tourneys, tournaments, 116.

Towardness, docility (the opposite of *forwardness*), 59.

Toy, a trifle, a thing of no serious importance, 57, 115, 116, 169.

Tract (of years), length, 128. *Tracts of his countenance*, features, play of features, 18.

Transcendences, imaginative flights, 15.

Trash, a contemptuous term for money, worldly goods, 39.

Travail, labour, 26 (here the original has "Travels").

Treaties, treatises, 9.

Trench to, trench on, touch, 165.

Tribunitious, like tribunes or demagogues, turbulent, 66.

Triumphs, shows or displays of some magnificence, 3, 134, and Essay xxxvii.

Troth, truth, 19.

Try it, enter on a contest (with), 60.

Tulippa, tulip, 137.

Turquets, ? Turkish dwarfs, 116.

Under foot, below the real value, 124.

Undertake, to take up (an affair), take in hand (said of a patron or person of influence), 148; cf. *undertakers*, 105.

Unproper, improper, unsuitable, 84.

Unsecreting, divulging, 63.

Uphold, make up for, balance (losses), 109

Upon (denoting the motive) = from, out of; *e.g. upon negligence* (87), *upon conscience*, etc. (114), *upon affection . . . upon discontentment* (146), *upon regard . . . upon facility* (155).

Upon (the foreigner), at the expense of, 45.

Upon speed, with speed, 108.

Upon recovery, on the point of recovering, 175.

Use, out of, out of practice, 19.

Use, usury, interest, 124. *Used*, practised, 33.

Value, put a high value on, recommend as men of substance, 109.

Vecture, carriage, carrying, 45.

Vein, inclination, disposition, 25, 102.

Vena porta; see Index of Phrases.

Ventureth, runs a risk, 131.

Version, turning, direction, 169.

Victual, victuals (the plural is used on same page), 104.

Vindicative, vindictive, 14.

Virtue, excellence of any sort in a man (not limited to moral virtue), 121, 129; so *virtuous*, of great parts, 41.

Vizars, masks, 116.

Voice, give voice to, proclaim, 32.

Voicing, giving out, proclaiming (that they are making good progress), 149.

Glossary

Votary (resolution), depending upon a vow, 119.

Vouched, adduced, 9.

Vulgar, common, applicable to many alike, 157.

Wait upon, watch, observe, 68, 108, 169; *waits upon his memory*, tries to recollect what he had to say, 76.

Wantons, spoilt children, 20.

Wardens, a kind of pear chiefly used for baking, 138.

Warm set, planted in a warm situation or aspect, 137.

Way, giveth best, best opens a way (to attaining one's object), 152; *keep way with*, keep pace with, 121. (See also *Put*.)

Weather, in, in rough weather, in a storm, 165.

Welts, borders, 140.

Wind of him, take the, play up to him, 66.

Wit, a great, a great intellect, a man of great intellectual powers, 131; cf. *discoursing wits*, 3.

With, a withy, an osier twig, 120.

Without himself, outside himself, 121.

Witty, ingenious, 9, 162; quick of fancy, 151.

Wood, in a, in a maze, 114.

Work, work upon, influence, 145.

Works, several, various designs, 135.

Would be, often = should be: *e.g. would be bridled*, ought to be bridled, 102; *this would be done*, 68; *care would be had*, 53.

Zelants, zealots, 9.